T0357763

TRY HARD

TRY
HARD

CREATIVE WORK IN PROGRESS

MAX
KERMAN

VIKING

VIKING

an imprint of Penguin Canada, a division of Penguin Random House Canada Limited

Canada • USA • UK • Ireland • Australia • New Zealand • India • South Africa • China

First published 2025

Viking, an imprint of Penguin Canada
A division of Penguin Random House Canada
320 Front Street West, Suite 1400
Toronto, Ontario, M5V 3B6, Canada
penguinrandomhouse.ca

The authorized representative in the EU for product safety and compliance is Penguin Random House Ireland, Morrison Chambers, 32 Nassau Street, Dublin D02 YH68, Ireland, https://eu-contact.penguin.ie

LIBRARY AND ARCHIVES CANADA CATALOGUING IN PUBLICATION

Title: Try hard : creative work in progress / Max Kerman.
Names: Kerman, Max, author.
Identifiers: Canadiana (print) 20240416538 | Canadiana (ebook) 20240417046 |
    ISBN 9780735248854 (hardcover) | ISBN 9780735248861 (EPUB)
Subjects: LCSH: Kerman, Max— Anecdotes. | LCSH: Rock musicians— Canada—
    Anecdotes. | LCSH: Singers— Canada— Anecdotes. | LCSH: Arkells (Musical
    group)— Anecdotes. | LCSH: Creative ability.
Classification: LCC ML420 .K395 A3 2025 | DDC 782.42166092— dc23

Cover and book design by Kate Sinclair
Cover illustrations by Tom Hill
Typeset in Bembo Book by Sean Tai

Printed in the United States of America

10 9 8 7 6 5 4 3 2 1

Penguin
Random House
VIKING CANADA

To the band: Anthony, Mike, Nick, and Tim.

CONTENTS

ENTERTAINMENT

I am not doing this for you, dear reader. I am doing this for me. This is the thing that artists and creatives rarely say but is obvious to me. For all the altruistic-sounding mentions of *community* and *connection* and the metaphysical ideas around *healing* and the *resiliency of the human spirit*, what creatives rarely acknowledge is this: *I am simply doing this for my own entertainment.*

It's January right now, and after a busy year of touring with my band, Arkells, I am home for a bit. I get the newspaper delivered in the morning and read it with my coffee. I go for walks and catch up with friends. I try to be a better uncle, son, and brother. But I am restless. Since I was a teenager, I've always been driven to pursue tangible goals. But it's only in the past few years that I've been able to keenly identify having a project as the thing that makes me tick.

Having a project on the go keeps me happy, fulfilled, and focused. When I don't have something to work toward, I get irritable. I get anxious. And that's how I'm starting to feel right now.

I have identified two times during the year when, like clockwork, I become irritable. It's the first three weeks of January and the last week of August. Nobody in the music business seems particularly interested in working, and fair enough. Emails are greeted with an out-of-office response, texts are slow, and I am *clearly* annoying everyone.

This type of malaise is my enemy. I imagine most people—regardless of their jobs—experience a version of this. It's a creeping sense of boredom or frustration with their daily work. But it's in the pursuit of not being bored that I'm almost always motivated to try something new. You might think, "Easy for you to say! You're the singer of a band. By definition, you have a fun job!" But most jobs—including my own—are kind of the same: you offer your spirit and talent, and you hope you can move the project or goal a little further up the road. I've come to learn that those who thrive demand that the work evolves and remains invigorating. I think this is the key.

I feel most alive when I'm involved in conversations about ideas. The size or commercial appeal of an idea is mostly irrelevant to me—and many of them go nowhere, but that's not the point. The point is the exercise itself. There is an electricity about a new idea that runs through me. Understanding how rewarding this feeling is, I end up seeking it out. It's a gift to have something to aspire to. But aspirations are rarely served up in a bow. I've got to find them. All day long, I am poking around in every conversation for something to light me up.

Beyond my unquestionable need for a project, the idea for this book came from a simple place: whenever I explain the nuts and bolts of my job to people I meet, they find it more interesting than I expect. Maybe a book could act as an extension of those conversations. Some people might even find it useful. And if I could write with the same enthusiasm I put into my daily work and lean into a key ingredient of anything I'm a part of—which is acquiring a lot of feedback from smart people that I trust—then I might be able to get the project to a place I can live with. Something I might be proud of.

I should note that the idea of writing a book originally seemed stupid to me because the premise was wrong. Who am I to write a book? Sure, I'm a guy in a band, and folks seem to like rock 'n' roll biographies. I do not. People assume that I have wild stories to share. I do not. Most daunting, there is a lot of agony and complaining involved in writing. The idea of locking myself away in some remote place to "write"—or to create anything for that matter—sounds terrible and isolating. Over the years I have been offered many cabins by friends to "get away from it all" so I can let my "creative juices fly," and I would simply prefer to *not*.

I like to be in the action. I like to bounce around and keep each moment of the day fresh until it's time for a nap around four p.m. As I conceived of the book, I began to think about how it might slot into my day. How would it make my day *feel*? What would I get out of it? Do I have the talent and patience for this? There were two anecdotes I kept going back to that changed my mind about writing a book and that I think get at something bigger about creative work.

The first is from my favourite writer, Michael Lewis, author of *The Big Short*, *Moneyball*, and the rest. I have read almost all his books, and I'm lucky to know him a bit as well. When I interviewed Michael on my podcast, he described his process in a way that made me feel like writing could be joyful. In fact, it sounds like a lively experience. Michael typically listens to music while he writes. He puts his headphones on and writes along to a playlist of "happy songs." (I've learned that Arkells have at times been included!) He told me that when his wife is within earshot, she hears him laughing while he's working, something he wasn't aware of. He's making sounds. He's reacting to the words he's creating on the page and does not hear himself laughing because of his headphones. What a nice thing to admit and an aspiring way to create.

The second is from Stephen King's book *On Writing*. I have never read a Stephen King novel nor do I know much about his movies. Horror scares me. But *On Writing* is about his literary process. I read it several years ago, and in it he explains something very simple that resonated: try to focus on a daily word count or number of pages per day. If you do this for a few months, you'll have enough words for a book. Simple math! Some days will be easy and the words will flow; others will be more challenging. But you will make progress just by starting. Word by word. He succinctly demystified his own work, describing straightforward and accessible strategies for any aspiring writer. He made me feel like any old fool could do it.

These two anecdotes embody the way I feel about creative work. First, it should be, to some degree, enjoyable. Michael Lewis reminds me that it's not against the rules to sometimes create with a smile on my face, whatever I'm doing. A kindred spirit. Stephen King reminds me to stop thinking about working and just start doing with a goal in mind each day.

As I began, my mind was consumed by writers and how they do it. Does a writer get inspired the same way a musician does? In my case, the effect of a great song is that it immediately draws me to the piano, inspiring me to write something of my own. Do authors react the same way? They must. While I'm a slow and often distracted reader, I have always admired writers—real writers—and their ability to make words jump off the page. I approached this project very humbly. I began writing with the hope that I could just get better. Writing with punch, brevity, and a voice that feels uniquely my own. But I wasn't inspired only by the greats; I also thought about my non-writer friends who rhyme off text messages in group chats with a prose style that is enviable.

So, here I am writing a book because, so far, I'm enjoying it even more than I thought I would. If the first 1,500 words had felt like a real inconvenience, I simply would've stopped. But quickly and unexpectedly, writing became a part of my day that I craved. It offered a new purpose. It gave me something to think about in the shower, waiting in line for a coffee, or walking through a park. It's been a great surprise in my life.

I know I came in hot off the top, explaining to you how this is for my own entertainment and how artists are kind of full of it when speaking of the healing power of art and creativity. But I wasn't being totally honest. While entertaining myself with this idea, other events began to unfold. What *was* originally an indulgent exercise revealed itself to be much more. It happens every time, and it feels like magic to me. The process goes like this:

1. I get pumped on an idea.
2. I start to fiddle with it.
3. I begin excitedly calling friends to workshop it.
4. Moments of connection, collaboration, and discovery inevitably follow.
5. All those lofty sayings about *community* and *resiliency* and *the human spirit* end up being true.

As you might be able to gather, there's real enthusiasm here for the project itself. I'm picking up steam! The title of the book—if you couldn't tell—is a double entendre. I thought it was funny. *Try hard* is traditionally a pejorative, like "Max is such a fucking try hard." I imagine some people might think that about me. But I have concluded that anyone who gets anywhere in this life is exactly that: a try hard. More to the point, if you have gone through the trouble of inventing a project for yourself, why wouldn't you try hard? So, I'm taking the term back. The title is also instructional. You must try hard to get anywhere, especially as a creative. Really hard. I don't know if being a creative person is a hard job, but it's a job where you must try hard.

I hope what's to come will entertain you. This is one of my goals. I'm also hoping that along the way, this book offers a path for anyone who wants to entertain themselves. If I can try something new, you can too. Maybe you're shy, or you think you're not good enough or don't have the talent to create something new. Or you're someone who wants to pursue a creative endeavour but might not know where to start. Start here: start with finding what entertains you and interact with those feelings. Just try it and see what happens.

LABELLING A "CREATIVE"

I am somewhat hesitant to define *creativity* for two reasons. First, there is already a litany of great books out there on the subject. Go read 'em! The genre is a cottage industry. Second (and this might feel a little more abstract), I find that language and labels—while meant to be useful—can be intimidating and unintentionally discouraging. Specifically, when it comes to creativity and the arts, there are certain grandiose words that get thrown around a lot—*transcendent*, *brave*, and even *artist*—that might feel foreign or hard to personally reconcile.

If you feel that way, you're not alone. Paul Simon, the great songwriter, had a hard time accepting the label "artist" until he was in his forties. For whatever reason, he didn't feel comfortable with it. Maybe he thought it was too grandiose.

Throughout his career, he just felt as if he was following his ear. As his music evolved and became more experimental, he continued to follow the sounds wherever they led him, and he wound up creating albums and learning from musicians in Alabama, South Africa, and Brazil. If Paul Simon had a hard time with the artist moniker, then I imagine it might be difficult for others to adopt the term themselves.

I relate to Paul Simon in that I don't consider myself an artist. For me, the term doesn't fit. When others apply it to themselves, I am unbothered. But the label and identity feel hard for me to square. I've been paying the bills as a musician for fifteen years, and yet I still have a hard time telling a stranger on a plane what my job is. "What do you do?" "Oh, I'm a musician." It sounds ridiculous to me. What I want to say is "Well, I have these cravings all day, every day, and I walk toward them. They are often about music or things related to promoting the music. But they really could be about anything."

I'm suspicious of tying anything too closely to identity, the composed list of things that make us who we are. In the beginning, when he was part of the duo Simon and Garfunkel, critics considered Paul Simon a folk artist in the vein of Bob Dylan, but somehow, despite their chart-topping acoustic songs, he never thought of himself that way. If he had considered himself strictly a folk singer, then we would never have heard the genre-defying album *Graceland*. He never allowed himself to be boxed in by his identity. He just followed his curiosity. There are pitfalls that come with labels, and Paul seemed to know that intuitively.

I prefer to talk about creativity in terms of action. When I think about any creative pursuit, I think of it as a very simple two-part equation: it's the recognition of something inside me that moves me and then the decision to move toward it. First, I feel preoccupied by an idea or an emotion that gives me butterflies—that's how I know I'm entertained—and then I decide to do something about it. In the simplest terms, it's not so different than craving a treat at three in the afternoon. Your brain goes, "I could use something sweet," and then you get off your couch and walk down the street to your favourite bakery to get a cookie. Or the decision to go for a walk when your body says, "I could use some fresh air." These analogies are useful to me because, like food and fresh air, I have different creative cravings throughout the day. I change the direction I'm moving in depending on my mood. When things aren't striking the right chord, I need to switch it up. Sometimes I move toward a piano. Sometimes I move toward my laptop to type something out. Sometimes I call a bandmate to ask a question. Sometimes I edit a video for social media.

The first part of the creativity equation—ideas and feelings—are things we all come by without even really trying. The second part, the act of *moving toward* those ideas and feelings, is harder for many and is the part of the equation that people sometimes don't do much about. A new pursuit can be jarring and intimidating. I get it. But to me, that feels like a pity, because there's so much fun to be had.

I know impressive people with wildly successful careers who look at my work with wonder, as if I'm speaking another language. "How do you write a song?" they ask. "I can't imagine writing a song!" I have heard this question not only from successful entrepreneurs but also from bestselling novelists. Huh? To me, those jobs seem much harder than what I do. What an artist does is something anyone can do. It's a set of skills that you *care* to build upon. That's it. The only difference between a songwriter and someone who hasn't written a song is that the artist has done the second part. They've walked toward the idea.

WORKING WITH
WHAT YOU'VE GOT

At the top of Kensington Market, the beloved eclectic neighbourhood in downtown Toronto, sits Major Street. That's where I grew up. It's sort of in the middle of everything. My parents moved to the street in 1980 and still live there to this day. My house was five hundred metres from my public school, which was right next to a legendary after-hours nightclub. It's six hundred metres from Chinatown, about nine hundred from Little Italy, and another five hundred to Little Portugal. On a bike, you could get to the SkyDome in ten minutes. It's a lively part of town. I'm biased, but I think it's the best street in the world. It's all right there. To this day, I crave the rhythm and action of a big city.

Lately, I've been thinking about my folks as they ease into retirement and I'm able to examine their lives with some newfound perspective. They've offered little gifts by virtue of their spirits that have guided me to where I am now. I imagine they don't even know it, but when I look closely, I can see that there are disparate, completely ordinary aspects of my life that I've learned are the key ingredients in how I see the world.

My dad was born and raised in a vaguely Jewish family on the Upper West Side in New York City. He is a trained social worker with a wide range of interests. He loves sports, follows politics, listens to podcasts, and exhibits many other typical dad behaviours. One day, he surprised us with a new hobby. He'd fallen in love with contra dancing, which he told us is a form of Scottish folk dancing. The man doesn't have a Scottish bone in his body. He had no prior dancing experience. But he loves it for the community, the exercise, and the music. What I see is that, even later in life, he's not afraid to try stuff. He's not afraid to be taken by a new idea. I admire his openness and appreciate how it's rubbed off on me.

Back in the late 1990s, he came across something called Conversation Café that had been invented by "some people in Seattle" and, for fun, thought he should be the person to bring the concept to Toronto. The premise was that anyone with a mind for civic engagement would meet at a public café for ninety minutes, and a leader would guide the group through a conversation, with the goal of helping to "make sense of the world." (That's literally on the website.) What a sweet idea. My dad's attempt to bring it to town was short-lived, as there wasn't enough interest, but he didn't feel particularly bothered that it didn't catch on. If you were to ask him today, he'd still believe it was an interesting idea worth pursuing. I must've picked up that instinct too. To not take things too personally, and to move along to the next idea when it's time.

My mum is from Toronto and grew up in a suburban, middle-class family. She eventually became a public high school teacher, a job she loved. At first glance, she's a cautious, rule-following person, but there are animated parts of her personality that continue to surprise me. She strikes up relationships with all kinds of people all over the neighbourhood. When we go out for coffee, her favourite baristas appear over the moon when she arrives to order her cortado. I'm the recognizable guy in a band, but she's the one getting the attention.

She never expected me to be a doctor, but I always had the sense that she hoped I'd find a path that offered some purpose. When I was in grade 9, I was surprised to find that I had been selected to be a member of a United Way youth leadership group with other high school students from across the city. At the time, I found it curious, as my grades were average and I didn't feel like a likely candidate for this high-achieving group. I couldn't tell you what we did or what was discussed, but I remember the kindness and enthusiasm of the older students who led the group. It felt special to be in their company, and the experience opened my eyes to students who shared community-minded goals. Years later, my mum mentioned that she had quietly signed me up for the group. I never knew. I wasn't picked because I was special; they just needed more kids involved, and my mum thought it might be good for me.

Recently on a walk, my mum proudly said, "You and your sister have such a genuine and lively relationship with life itself." Of all the ways a parent could offer a compliment, this felt the most meaningful. It had nothing specifically to do with our careers or accomplishments; it was just about how we go about interacting with the world.

LAZY

When I was fifteen, I had a hunch that I might not be lazy. So far in high school, I'd been able to skate through school with okay grades, without applying much effort. I played sports, but if they stressed me out, I was happy to walk away. I don't know if anyone would have called me ambitious or serious. I was a very normal directionless teen. But one day, I ended up stumbling across something that surprised me. Sitting underneath the living room cabinet was my dad's dusty acoustic guitar case, and I opened it up and decided to painstakingly learn a few chords. I started with "Eight Days a Week." Learning that I might be able to play a Beatles song meant so much to me and felt unlike anything else. I could barely believe it. All of a sudden there was a new feeling running parallel to my objectively lazy behaviour.

Without much intention, my life became a cycle that revolved around music and songwriting. I went from quitting piano lessons four years earlier and neglecting the slightly out-of-tune upright piano in my family's living room to playing almost every day. I had never been good at piano, but I started again with a new approach. I learned some simple chords to serve the Beatles songs I was practising, which in turn inspired my own songs. Turns out, all I needed was a few chords to get started. I was either at home practising guitar and piano, or I was jamming with other neighbourhood kids who were also learning to play. And when I didn't have an instrument in my hand, I was *thinking* about my own songs.

The early songs I wrote were varied in tone and form. The first one I wrote on the guitar was inspired by my first girlfriend. It featured a simple progression that my dad showed me—the only three chords he knew—where I hardly had to move my fingers from the D chord. It was a sentimental acoustic ballad, poetically named "Coolest Girl Ever." Then there was a piano rocker about my geography teacher, an eccentric man named Mr. Kuehn, famous for smoking indoors and warring with the administration, aptly named "Crazy Ol' Kuehn." I later played it for the entire school at an assembly, and he loved it, appearing onstage with a box on his head mid-song.

These were all ideas that excited me, and I knew the next step was to figure out how to record them. One weekend, I went to Steve's Music Store on Queen Street West in downtown Toronto and rented a digital recorder for three days.

This was before user-friendly programs like GarageBand became commonplace, and the complicated machine intimidated me. The recording gear seemed quite intricate, and I'd never been good at following steps in an IKEA-build-it-yourself kind of way. To this day, if there's a task in front of me that feels too complex, I get frustrated immediately. It becomes a game of "How do I get out of this assignment?" But that weekend something felt different.

I became obsessed with figuring out how to use the device so I could record my songs. The equipment I'd rented was mobile but clunky, and I brought it over to my neighbours where we played music in the basement. Alex and Eli Keleher were brothers who lived across the street and their mom, Leslie—who was far more adoring and patient with her kids than my own mother was—allowed us to make a racket and jam.

With Eli on the drums and Alex on electric guitar, the brothers backed me up so we could demo my songs. They'd indulge me before heading upstairs for dinner, leaving me to listen back to what we'd just done. I sat in their basement for hours, trying to figure out how to overdub additional parts and harmonies, to get the songs sounding just right. I suddenly possessed an unrecognizable laser focus and resolve. The assignment felt like second nature. It didn't feel like work at all. This, I learned, was a form of love. When you're passionate about something, you'll go to the moon and back to figure it out.

Beyond figuring out the device, I was learning to delineate between the part of music-making that I enjoyed—the songwriting—and the part I disliked—the recording. Songwriting offered a new path for me. It was cathartic. It gave me something to think about at any hour of the day. It was a form of self-expression that helped make sense of my feelings. It could give me an excuse to perform for a crowd. And most significantly, it offered an assignment I was *actually* interested in completing.

However, the recording process wasn't pretty—that device was a land mine of confusion. Most recording software is still too elaborate for me. Despite the laser focus I had on my first attempt, I soon learned that I would much rather delegate the task to a professional. I am envious of musicians who can find joy in writing and producing and engineering all at once, and I wish I could be more like that. As it stands right now, I spend most of my life trying to avoid the more technical parts of being a musician. But as a teen, I was beaming from my accomplishment. I had been rewarded with the satisfaction of putting my feelings and ideas into songs *and* sharing them with others.

There was a mix of idealism and curiosity and vanity in my formative songwriting pursuits. First, it was a tool for romance. Not many other kids were writing songs as gifts for their crushes. A competitive advantage. But I also desperately wanted to hear my own voice back—and to admire what I had created from a distance. When I finally did hear my voice on my recordings, I was not happy. It wasn't how I heard it in my head. It was nasal and high-pitched. It sounded nothing like any of my favourite singers. My imagined voice was something that could lead to stardom, but my actual voice made me shudder. But this issue—a shit voice—didn't discourage me. It made me want to compensate for it with what I felt I could control. The compositions would have to be stronger. The lyrics would need to be more striking. My performance on stage would need to be more compelling—all things I still believe today. I figured if I kept doing all those things, there was a chance my voice would gradually change. Maybe through puberty, that teenaged nasally thing would grow into something more appealing.

By the time I had returned the recorder, songwriting was the only thing on my mind.

That winter, I encountered my first job in a long string of 'em that I was completely ambivalent about. I worked at Trinity Bellwoods Park as a rink guard at the public skating rink. This remains a funny job to me because I still can't really skate. I can glide forward, but I can't stop or go backwards. Thankfully, ice time did not matter, as I was distracted by my newfound hobby. I remember being huddled inside the change room office, stressing myself out to no end about how to finish my next song. I had just completed one called "Tragic Flaw" (which five years later ended up on Arkells' first album, *Jackson Square*) and was so pleased with the result that I was worried, at the age of sixteen, that I might've peaked.

Besides opening the rink in the morning, I barely went outside. I hunkered down in the tiny shack next to the skating rink, flipped through the occasional *Maxim* magazine left behind by the other rink guards, and obsessed over the details of my writing. I remember my uncertainty as I worked through a chord progression that I worried felt too predictable. There was the agony of working on lyrics that felt honest and heart-felt, but also some version of cool. But as it turned out, these were problems I was determined to engage with. As I worked and waited for my next song to feel complete, amid my stress, I didn't realize that I was already living a life that revolved around the project itself. Stress, I learned, meant that I cared. And caring about something was a feeling I began to revere.

If you asked any of my former bosses if I was a good employee, the answers would be the same: nice kid but lacks any real elbow grease. I worked at countless jobs—an ice cream parlour, a coffee shop, a restaurant—and it was all the same. I was always a few minutes late. Laissez-faire about the rules. Impatient. Bad at cleaning up. The customers usually liked me, but I was not technically good at my job. If you asked me to make a latte or a cappuccino or a flat white, I'd make them all same way—espresso + some foamy milk—and serve them up with a smile. It wasn't because I wasn't capable; I just didn't care to learn the difference. And when I didn't care about something, the details didn't matter to me.

When you get lost headlong in a new creative passion, no one tells you about the amount of learning, second-guessing, and general stress that might follow, but I've learned that these are feelings you shouldn't fear. There are inner struggles that you experience as a songwriter that will always exist. But if you're consumed by an idea, the path is simple: you toil away at it until it feels right.

The inkling that I might not be lazy was a revelation. Even to this day, I have a hard time completing anything that I am not interested in. I get sleepy. Ask me to do a chore around the house and I need a nap. My body shuts down. What I couldn't see at the time was that songwriting consumed me in the way that sports, my first love, had consumed me as a child. For the first time in a while, I felt as if I really cared about what I was doing. It showed me that I wasn't unwilling to work; I just hadn't found the thing that moved me to action. In trying to complete a song, I learned something about myself.

MEET THE BAND

In 2004, as I was finishing high school, I began to romanticize what university would look like. My high school bandmates were heading to different colleges, but somehow I wasn't discouraged. I assumed there would be many new like-minded people beyond the borders of my own neighbourhood that I'd meet in short order. I had pulled together decent-enough grades to be accepted by two schools, but in my mind, I was going to university for one reason: to start a band. The plan always made sense in my head. I'd make my mum happy and get a degree, but I'd find a band. That was the point. I planned to take some wishy-washy social sciences courses that I guessed required little academic rigour, so my imagined band and I would have lots of time to write songs and play gigs.

Like any good story that works out, the way things unfolded appears more preordained than it felt in the moment. I didn't know that the guys I'd meet would help shape the rest of my life. I didn't fully understand how talented they were or that our instincts and goals would align as well as they did. But I did understand that I couldn't pull off more than a few lo-fi basement recordings on my own. Maybe it's an instinct that comes from my love of team sports. Like with a basketball or baseball team, I intuitively knew that if I was going to build a creative team—a band—then I'd need talent in every department. So, when I got to McMaster University in Hamilton, that's exactly what I set out to find.

Frosh week offered the perfect scouting opportunity. What happens during frosh week isn't that different than schmoozing, which you end up doing a fair amount of in the music business. Students, often away from home for the first time, share a spirit of palpable optimism about their futures, while trying to hide their palpable desperation to make new friends. But unlike the industry events I'd become familiar with later, where there's a certain amount of posturing, everyone at university that first week was in the same boat. Everyone was new. It was in everyone's interest to be friendly. Extroverts like me did just fine, but even introverts put on a brave face and came out of their shells for the week. Once classes began, I knew students would settle into their friend groups, so I tried to get ahead of things during the first week and seize the opportunity to find a band. *Everyone* was a potential bandmate, and I didn't waste any time.

I went into each social interaction with a sincere desire to understand other people—what excited them and what their interests were. Looking back, I came by this assignment honestly. I am by nature a very trusting person, and I tend to like most people on first impression. I don't have my guard up at all, and I think it allows others to let their guard down in return. Despite some belief in my songwriting and performing, I feel like my main talent is enthusiasm. I assume everyone I meet is smarter, more talented, and more diligent than me.

With crowds of people shuffling all over campus, I had to find a way to narrow down the potential candidates. I started by profiling people in the most basic way: I looked for people whose hair looked dishevelled. Musicians—at least the ones I wanted to meet—traditionally had longer hair that reflected their musical taste in indie rock. At the time, my hair was one big ball of puffy curls, contained by an old-fashioned train conductor hat I modelled after John Lennon's signature look from the *A Hard Day's Night / Help!* era—a reference *nobody* got. If they were also wearing a band T-shirt, I assumed there was a chance they'd be the kind of person who'd want to play in a band.

I'd walk up to any party and make my best attempt at polite conversation before getting to the task at hand. I had a two-part quiz prepared. First question: "What kind of music do you like?" If they answered *correctly*, according to my specific tastes, they'd get the follow-up: "Do you play an instrument?"

I had learned from my high school bands that I didn't want to spend time arguing about what kind of music we'd play. There had been some neighbourhood kids who only wanted to play Pink Floyd and Led Zeppelin, and my reaction was always "Count me out." I had a sense of the kind of band I wanted to be in. Hooky melodies with a pop sensibility, shimmering electric guitars, big drums—something that would get a crowd moving. I figured if I could bond with someone over a shared love of the same music, then the commitment to writing our own songs would come next.

I can't tell you how many people I met who didn't fit the bill. Sometimes the person in question would look the part, but they only wanted to talk about their love for Metallica. No thank you. Sometimes there would be a mutual love of The Beatles, but they couldn't play an instrument. Sometimes they could play an instrument but were enrolled in the music program and had little interest in being in a rock band.

On the second day, at a mixer by the football field, I met a guy who lived in the residence building next to mine. His name was Mike DeAngelis. I did my song and dance again. Mike D., thoughtful with his words, explained that he liked a lot of different styles of music, but the band he liked the most at that moment was a smaller act from Winnipeg that I "probably hadn't heard of."

"They're called The Weakerthans. Do you know them?"

I couldn't believe what I was hearing. Over the previous year, The Weakerthans had become one of my favourite bands. They were fronted by a thoughtful Winnipegger named John

K. Samson. He had a nasally voice (that gave me hope for my own), and his band had grown a small and mighty army of followers. His lyrics were poetic, brimming with academic and historical references. The songs felt smarter than a lot of the other popular music at the time. The Weakerthans had become darlings of the Canadian punk and indie rock scene, but they weren't a band you'd hear on the radio or see on the television. They felt like my secret.

I literally pushed Mike in the chest and cried out, "I love The Weakerthans! They're my favourite band!" Mike almost fell over, responding to my hysteria with a confused smile. I explained that I had travelled to Hamilton with my dad that summer to see them perform at a small rock club called the Underground.

I collected myself and asked him the next question. This one could be the deal breaker.

"Do you play an instrument?"

"Well. Hmmm. I sort of play the guitar."

"You're in the band!"

"Oh! Well, I'm not particularly good. But I have a little practice amp at home and a Squier Stratocaster. I could get it next time I'm back home in Guelph? Also, what band?"

"Great. We will figure it out. Can't wait."

The next afternoon as I exited the stairwell of my residence, Brandon Hall, I was stopped by a friendly guy who complimented my shirt. He was tall, dark, and handsome and had a sweetness that I felt instantly. I was wearing a Sam Roberts Band T-shirt that I had purchased the week before at his Toronto concert. Sam Roberts was the hottest new rock 'n' roll act in the country, and I loved his debut record, *We Were Born in a Flame*.

"Thank you! I'm Max. I love Sam Roberts Band. I just saw them. Do you like them?"

"I'm Nick. Ya, they're great."

I got right to the point: "Do you play an instrument?"

"Well, I sort of play bass. I did in high school."

"You're in the band," I said.

His full name was Nick Dika.

That's how it started.

THE FIRST SHOWS

No one ever gets where they want to be immediately. There are no straight lines, and so much education happens at every turn if you're paying attention. Before Arkells became who we are today, we were just a few guys trying to find ways to keep making music. It looked quite different than it does today. We had early members who were replaced. We even had a different name, Charlemagne, plucked from a textbook in some first-year university class.

Nick, Mike D., and I began rehearsing as a trio in Mike's dorm room. His neighbours complained about the noise, the residence staff were called, and we were told that we had to stop. We then moved to the centrally located common room on the ground floor of his residence, and the whole building complained. We were briefly allowed to use a room in the music department, but it was mostly reserved for students who enrolled in the program. Our stay ended after one session. The message was clear: the music room was for *real* musicians, not our band. But the great thing about playing in a band is that it doesn't have to be perfect. Regardless of our proficiency, the chemistry felt original, and I felt that we could musically grow together.

Nick and Mike were academically inclined and generally more interested in being in school than I was. I quickly learned of the studying commitments from friends enrolled in various faculties. It seemed engineering students did nothing but work. Same with the science kids. Friends in humanities and social sciences, on the other hand, seemed to have plenty of time on their hands. Mike, Nick, and I took many of the same classes, so I had a hunch they might have time for the band. Luckily, we were all on track for a political science degree. If they had been preparing for med school, I don't know if the band would've worked.

By January, we found a drummer in Mike's residence building—a perfectly nice guy who owned a drum kit—and our unit began to rehearse in earnest as we eyed the annual campus battle of the bands that happened during the spring semester.

The event was held at the campus bar called Quarters, and each band was permitted a three-song set. On the day of the show, we realized we didn't have a way to transport our equipment, so we picked up a grocery cart that had been left for dead outside our residence and hauled it the five hundred yards across campus. Our friends all showed up to support, and we put on a fiery ten-minute set. All the songs, sounds, and stage moves were inspired by the bands we loved at the time. We placed first that night, advancing to the final the following month, where we were runners-up to a ska band. The validation propelled us.

One of our early out-of-town gigs was booked in Nick's hometown of London, Ontario. Once again, we had no travel options. It was two hours away by car, and no one was offering a lift. Assessing our options, and realizing there was only one, we purchased tickets for a Greyhound bus and put our gear in the undercarriage. The show was attended by fifteen of Nick's childhood friends, and we stayed at his parents' house before getting on the bus to head back to Hamilton the next morning.

By third year, we'd expanded to a five piece after meeting a talented keyboardist named Dan Griffin. Seeing potential in our band, he quickly encouraged us to find a drummer with more experience and care and suggested a friend of his named Tim Oxford. We felt the results right away, with the band achieving a new level of musicianship and songwriting. The work became more intense, as we booked as many gigs as we could and plotted recording time for our first EP. If we had a show in Toronto, we'd load up Dan's small sedan with as much gear as we could, and the rest of us would hop on the express bus that runs from Hamilton to Toronto. We'd arrive at Union Station, take the subway or streetcar to the venue, and help unload the gear.

None of this stuff felt ridiculous at the time. All of it felt like something that we simply had to do. If we had gone through the trouble of booking a gig and working with a local promoter or band in another city, then we had to figure out how to get to the show. Despite the duct-taped approach to our early gigs, we were deadly serious about making the most of each one.

IT'S AN ECOSYSTEM

Once you get going in a creative collaboration, there are so many things that need to be tended to. What starts out as a solo endeavour becomes an ecosystem and keeping everything in balance winds up being more essential than you might realize. Over the years, early band members parted ways, and managers changed, but the pursuit remained the same. Who do you want to share the trip with? And who wants to share the trip with you?

I've shared so many experiences with Mike D. and Nick. Sometimes it's hard to believe we've known each other for more than half my lifetime. But the three of us would all admit that we're not technically skilled musicians and that enthusiasm can only get you so far. When we met Tim, and Anthony Carone a few years after that, the chemistry of the group felt like it fell into place. Both brought in a level of musicianship that we lacked and were like-minded in their pursuit of wanting to find a band to call home. If we were five lead singers or five drummers, it wouldn't have worked, but we found a way for everyone to slot into a role that suited their talents.

If you're lucky to find people to fill the missing pieces, you find a way to bring them into the conversation. Before long, you might start to wonder how you ever lived without them. When you find collaborators who enjoy what they're doing, then you might have some longevity.

The first time we jammed with Tim, the power and precision of his playing made us sound like a real rock 'n' roll band. In short order, Tim volunteered to record our demos in his parents' basement. Despite my early forays into recording, I still had no real interest in audio engineering, but Tim had studied music production in college and was willing and capable. With his own gear, he helped produce better-sounding recordings than anything we had ever made. That's the power of collaboration. All of a sudden, our scrappy little songs felt more professional because of Tim.

Anthony studied jazz at Humber College and can speak a musical language the rest of us cannot. We all admire his stage presence, but his knowledge of music theory has been equally important. Not only can he produce string and horn arrangements, charting out scores for each additional guest musician, he helps the rest of the band make sense of my often-blurry creative visions. Sometimes it's comically rudimentary stuff, but we'd be lost without him. I'll suggest an idea that is met with blank stares, and Anthony is there to interpret my ramblings and set things right: "Guys, I think he wants you to play a C instead of a D."

Even though I'm the frontman, I don't see my job as more important than the other moving parts happening around me. *It's all important*. But most important of all, I couldn't do it alone. I am often the driver of ideas and plans, but I rely on their feedback to sharpen concepts or to tell me when something's not worth pursuing.

The number one thing I tell any young creative: find talented co-conspirators whom you admire and go on the journey with them. Find people who have skills that you don't. Grow together. The reciprocal nature of these relationships can lift everyone involved.

Like any relationship, the dynamic between the five of us is constantly evolving, but it's largely been a functional and supportive unit. We learned a lot about each other over the years, especially in the early days. While those first shows felt like one big adventure, there was a toll that came with touring in a van and sharing motel rooms. The future was so uncertain. Money was tight, diets were terrible, and we were all under-slept. We share that history. Like any family unit, we're prone to get on each other's nerves. But I know a good thing when I see it. I have a goal for us to age like one of those married couples that still likes each other. As time goes on, everyone has had the good sense to try and understand each other's strengths and insecurities. We all do our best to keep the ecosystem healthy and meet each other where we are.

The nature of the relationship is truly unlike anything else. We are friends. We are colleagues. We own a business together. We are individual artists trying to express ourselves in relation to each other. And we started working together when we were teenagers. It's unique for all those reasons, but I think we recognize that's exactly what makes it special.

FAMILY "BUSINESS"

The influence of your family can permeate in different and subtle ways throughout your life. With time, I've learned my job as singer in a band parallels my dad's career path in a myriad of ways. And none of them have to do with music. There is a connection between creativity and entrepreneurship that is more harmonious than most would imagine. I like to think I've followed in my dad's footsteps to make my passion a career.

Michael Kerman is not a musician or a songwriter. He is a trained social worker. In my childhood, I do remember him composing *one song*: a very amateur eight-bar blues riff on the piano, played with three fingers, pleading with his children to put on their shoes and get in the *fucking* car. He'd playfully sing, "I got the blues! 'Cause my children won't get in the car!"

In 1992, my dad, a good-natured, dutiful person, had had enough of his job—so he invented a new one. At forty-six, he was the director of a social services agency called YouthLink that ran group homes for troubled teenagers. He enjoyed the job in many ways. My dad was and continues to be an easygoing, sweet kind of leader. The staff were his friends, and he had all the right kinds of compassion for the youth who ended up in these difficult circumstances. But anyone who works in social services will tell you that it's not the clientele that might dim your spirit; it's the bureaucracy. After twenty years in the field, he was burnt out and asking himself if this was really the way he wanted to spend his time.

The plan for his new business combined all his interests. As a social guy, he liked being around people. As a leader, he wanted to nurture an environment for people to come together. As a lifelong student of the mental health profession, he wanted to learn more. So, he hatched a plan to open Leading Edge Seminars, a business to facilitate continuing education training for mental health professionals. I describe the job to my friends by saying he's like a concert promoter for therapists. He finds the star act, books them for an event, and people buy tickets to the show.

What led him on this new path was an act of innovation itself. As the director at YouthLink, part of his job was organizing continuing education for his staff. Continuing education is often a requirement for ongoing development in professional fields. If you had written a book with fresh ideas about marriage counselling, addiction treatment, or handling clients with PTSD, my dad might enlist you to run a training session for his team. Through this experience, he realized there might be a small opening in the market for continuing education. It would be a very niche business, but a business.

It's common for titans of business to encourage entrepreneurs to find that billion-dollar idea missing in the marketplace, but my dad wasn't driven by such ambitions. He just wanted to do something that he enjoyed and figured that if he could do it well enough, the rest would sort itself out. This sense of optimism is hard to come by, but as a creative, it feels essential.

From there, he invented a business model. Long before we knew the term *work from home*, he operated out of our house to save money on renting an office. My mum, a trained freelance graphic designer, was responsible for making the brochures to promote the workshops. He built up a database of mental health agencies, sent out the flyers, and crossed his fingers that folks would sign up. He eventually hired staff that worked out of our house during the day.

There is a small business attitude that requires some imagination, and I began picking up thrifty tricks by observing his day-to-day life. Saving money was important. My dad never got a second phone line for the house, so if my sister, Emily, and I were home between nine and five during the week, we were expected to answer the phone with a professional "Hello, you've reached Leading Edge Seminars. How may I help you?" The person on the other end would inevitably ask for Michael Kerman, and we'd put down the phone receiver and yell, "DAD!!!!!!"

Early on, the workshops were a family affair. During the week leading up to the Friday conference, my dad would set up a workstation on our dining room table with all the materials that his guests would receive for an assembly-line-style production. It was simple work that I—a seven-year-old—could perform, alongside Emily. We'd take stacks of stapled material, file them into binders, and put them into boxes. When we were all finished, we'd load them into our 1986 Toyota Camry hatchback.

If the conference was a big one, he'd take my sister and me out of school for the morning, and we'd help set up the facility he had rented out. We'd leave the house in the dark at six a.m. to get the coffee going, the muffins and croissants laid out, and the registration table ready for the patrons. With some distance, it was not that different from loading in gear at a concert venue and setting up your T-shirts at the merch booth.

You can draw a line between this practice and the all-for-one spirit of being in a band. Before Arkells ever officially manufactured a real album, we'd buy a fifty stack of blank CDs from the computer store, burn our new songs at home, and stuff them in envelopes from the post office, so we'd have music to sell at the next gig. Today, before a new album comes out, the band lines up as an assembly line, signing stacks of vinyl records. And it all reminds me of my first gig at Leading Edge Seminars.

There is no boss telling you how hard to work when you're running your own shop. Figuring out how to juggle life and work commitments is something every adult must contend with, but when you're inventing your own pursuit, the discipline required is that much more important. For Leading Edge Seminars to have a chance, my parents had to adjust to a lack of conventional structure and find small compromises that would support both the business and our family. If you can imagine ways to bend the world to your will—shorten your commute, have your family tag in—it'll make everything a little easier. When Arkells started touring, no one *wanted* to work a part-time job—we just wanted to make music and play shows—but that's the way it had to be if we wanted to make rent.

When I recently mentioned to my dad that I get irritable at the beginning of January, he said, "It starts on December twenty-eighth for me!" There is an all-encompassing nature to the way he works that he can't quite shut off. But I don't think he'd call himself a workaholic. If anything, he takes so much pleasure in his day-to-day because it's completely on his own terms. He constantly finds delight in the little things. When we discuss the band and what I'm up to, it's no different. It's the small, unexpected experiences that I stumble into that really get him excited.

Over the last few winters, there has been a vote to name the local snowplows in Hamilton, Ontario. Names were submitted by city staff, and anyone could vote. Believe it or not, one year "Max Kermanator" won by a landslide with over eighteen thousand votes. Second place was "Plowy

McPlowface," arriving short of three thousand votes. This was of course very silly, but nobody was happier about the whole thing than my dad. Not because our family name was on a snowplow, but because of how profoundly amusing the whole thing was. It was in the newspaper and shared online. He kept messaging me about how I should hold a campaign event and give an Obama-style speech thanking my supporters. I did not do these things, but now you have a sense of where I get my penchant for a bit, and the unexpected places I find joy in my job.

LUCK

Luck. What is that thing, really? Sometimes I'm asked about when Arkells got our "lucky big break." I can tell that people want to hear the story of an eye-opening mystical moment when the cosmos aligned and we found ourselves in an unlikely scenario to which we attribute our success. For them, luck often feels completely separate from the basic work, passion, and curiosity that led to those "lucky" moments in the first place.

Looking back, I can point to a few instances when it felt like our career really turned a corner, but the more honest answer is that there were a number of smaller, less awe-inspiring moments that built our success along the way. I didn't always recognize the small successes that would catapult us forward in the moment, but when I look back, I can draw a line from one event to the next, and I see how they helped us get where we are today. Any defining moment is often the sum of its parts, and while there are no guarantees, it starts with taking advantage of opportunities when they present themselves.

To understand the story of our "big break," and the unexpected ways things can build on each other and connect, I would need to draw you a road map of about five years that includes many stops and starts along the way.

In high school you could find me wandering around the hallways with my acoustic guitar, singing cover songs that nobody asked for. To this day, if you ask kids I went to high school with if they have any memory of me, it's this vision: me singing parody songs on the morning announcements, enjoying myself, and trying to avoid class. I had two very supportive teachers—Ms. Garner-Pringle and Ms. Reinis—who both happened to be married to partners working in the Toronto music industry. I can't recall *how* I found out my teachers had these connections, but at the time I had aspirations to break into the music business, and I made it clear to anyone within earshot. When I have an idea in mind, I talk about it often, hoping that someone might be able to help connect some dots. These teachers must've had a soft spot for me, because when I asked if they could put me in touch with their partners about a volunteer position, they obliged.

They referred me to a music booking agency called The Agency Group. It was one of the headquarters of live music in Canada with a roster of agents booking shows for artists spanning every genre, from Feist to Nickelback to Great Big

Sea. I sent off a couple of emails, and I was soon connected to the boss, Jack Ross, for an interview.

When I walked into the building, I felt the electricity of the music business in its walls. I sat in Jack's corner office on the second floor in awe of the platinum records, framed prints of arena shows, personal backstage photos, and memorabilia that surrounded us. My parents never worked in an office, so this all felt new. I tried to keep my focus as Jack told me what the job would entail. He explained I'd be able to work my other job at the ice cream parlour, but two afternoons a week that summer I'd be expected to help file show contracts. I'd also be on call to help the other agents with whatever they needed. The pay would be an honorarium of $50 a week. I didn't blink—I said yes immediately.

You might think filing contracts sounds like a pretty boring way to spend a summer. But as I sat on the floor outside Jack's office and sorted paperwork, I began to learn the ins and outs of the music industry. Sam Roberts was just establishing himself as a star, and I quickly learned what a festival offer might look like. Matt Mays and El Torpedo, another client, was on tour with Blue Rodeo, and I began to understand how an opening act might get booked. There were days when Jack would bring his dog to the office and take us both out for walks, regaling me with stories. Other times, a younger agent, Adam Countryman, would take me under his wing, treat me to a coffee, and field all of my burning questions. Each day offered a new lesson about the music industry.

When Arkells got together and started booking gigs and making demos, I reached out to Jack and Adam to see if they wanted to work with our band. We were young and new, and I knew that *a great artist needs a great team around them*—that's what Jack and Adam had taught me. I wrote them the minute our band accomplished *literally anything*. The first time we recorded a song in our friend's basement: "Check it out!" The first time we booked our own show in Guelph: "You'd be proud!" All these years later, Jack insists the office had been keeping an eye on our development. But a few other things would have to come together before they'd take us seriously.

After our third year of university, we had made incremental improvements to our songwriting and live show, but I was still somewhat unsure that the band would exist beyond university. When Tim had joined the band, we were surprised to learn his drum teacher was Jeremy Taggart (of Our Lady Peace), who later helped mentor the band and provided invaluable support. But beyond that, few other industry players seemed to take much note.

That summer, we had booked a gig at North by Northeast (NXNE) in Toronto. It was a real festival, and our name would be in print on the festival poster beneath the big headlining acts. Landing the festival felt like the result of a lot of hustle. Between classes and part-time jobs, we had developed a good group work ethic, making friends with local bands and promoters from Southern Ontario, trying to establish ourselves from the ground up.

At the time, it felt like the opportunity of a lifetime, so we dressed for the occasion. Inspired by our love of Americana and roots rock—classic stuff like Neil Young and The Band— we all wore second-hand cream-coloured cowboy shirts that we bought at Value Village. We normally didn't dress alike—and I don't think we have since—but we did on that day.

On that hot June afternoon, in a public space that had seen crowds of fifteen thousand people, we took the stage and played a raucous forty-minute set for an audience of roughly twenty-five, including my sweet grandmother who was sitting on the seat of her walker. It was the first and only gig of mine she ever attended. The outdoor afternoon show was more suitable for her than the grimy club gigs we normally played.

Afterwards, we felt pretty good about the show despite the turnout. We tried to lean into the little wins: our instruments were in tune, and we were getting more confident as performers. When I went to the merch booth, it turned out we'd sold a handful of freshly pressed copies of our brand-new, self-produced, and self-funded EP. We left with the satisfaction that we'd played an actual festival.

What we didn't know that day was that a fellow named Shawn Creamer happened to be hungover and walking by the stage after eating his breakfast. Shawn was the owner and operator of the Dakota Tavern, a basement bar and intimate live-music venue located in Toronto's west end where many of the city's musicians and industry folks live. He listened to our band from the back of the square and bought six copies of our EP. *Six*. He took them to the bar across town and kept them handy in case he encountered a patron in need of some new music. For reasons that are still perplexing to me, Shawn took it upon himself to give our EP to managers and record label folks he felt might connect with the music. It seemed like a simple, generous act for no other reason than he's a generous person.

A few months later we got a message out of the blue from Joel Carriere, the owner of Dine Alone Records and Bedlam Music Management, an indie label that was home to some of the most notable names in Canadian indie rock, including Alexisonfire, City and Colour, and Bedouin Soundclash. He explained how he'd got his hands on our EP and was intrigued from the first lyric, "Oh, the boss is coming!" He told us he liked what he heard and wanted to see us play live. We understood this could be a big deal, a turning point for us. Having someone well-respected like Joel in our corner was something we needed.

This might appear to be a discernable moment of luck, but it was the result of all the things that came before it. We weren't up there swinging haphazardly. If you're improving on your craft *and* keep going up to bat, someone will eventually take notice. To stumble into some luck, each step must be a deliberate one.

We wound up playing a showcase of sorts at the Dakota Tavern the next month, graciously arranged by Shawn. Joel and his right-hand man, Nathan Stein, came to check us out. I don't remember much about the gig, except that the stage was tiny and there were about ten people watching. But it was enough for Joel to want to work with us. We were off to the races.

A full-circle moment happened shortly thereafter. With Joel as our manager, the next step was securing a booking agent, and lucky for us, most of Joel's acts were booked out of The Agency Group. This is the way it often works in the music biz: if you want to work with a manager on their big acts, you're often obliged to take on their developing artists. In our case, if you wanted to work with Joel's established bands, then you had to also work with Arkells. Jack and Adam naturally became our agents. The luck of working with Jack and Adam, my two former bosses, felt like having a security blanket with us as we entered the next phase of our career.

Anyone who's found some commercial success has a version of this story. I sometimes think about what would have happened if Shawn Creamer hadn't walked by Yonge-Dundas Square that day. How would our career be different? If luck existed, it had just as much to do with our ongoing hustle as it did with any collision with serendipity.

DISTRACTIONS

When we started working with our first manager, Joel, and he agreed to put out our albums on his label, we were thrilled. The timing was perfect. We were just finishing university, so our next "life decision" had been made for us. We didn't have to worry about finding grown-up jobs or applying to grad school. We had a plan: go on tour, put out our debut record, and cross our fingers that an audience would discover us. We assumed that if we did all this correctly, we'd be able to make music our full-time career.

What we *didn't* know was how important momentum can be. We didn't fully understand how much time and attention ought to be spent on each area of our operation. During this period, I developed a feeling that I'd later come to understand most artists experience. I began to notice what felt like an internal radar gun, monitoring the velocity of our career. As an artist, sometimes it feels like your career is going too fast, and other times it feels like it's grinding to a halt. I've come to recognize that each part of our creative evolution and business operation moves along at its own pace but is ideally cruising at a comfortable speed. Most of the time, the way you perceive your career correlates with the compatibility of your team.

Things became complicated after our 2009 showcase at South by Southwest (SXSW) in Austin, Texas. We were the belle of the ball at that festival, and every major and indie label wanted to sign us. It was a very exciting time, and I don't think we realized how unique the kind of attention we received was. We were only twenty-two, and everything— specifically the fate of our long-term future as a band— seemed to be happening at once.

Things began to fall apart with Joel when it came down to choosing which international label we'd sign with. Atlantic Records was at the top of the list, and their A&R reps—the label staff responsible for signing and nurturing talent—were in hot pursuit of us. Following SXSW, they flew to Whistler, B.C.; London, U.K.; and Hamilton, ON, to see Arkells perform and attempted to familiarize the band with how our working relationship might look. They wanted to demonstrate that they were serious about being in business with Arkells and spared no expense doing so. Eventually, we flew to New York City to visit their office and meet the entire team, before a fancy dinner and a night out at the Blue Note, the legendary jazz club.

We were having trouble making a decision, as the details of the deal felt increasingly complicated. A new business model had taken hold of the music industry, called a 360 deal, which meant that the label would be involved in *all* parts of our business. Traditionally, labels made their money by selling music, and that was it. But with the rise of digital streaming and diminishing return on album sales, labels insisted on participating in other revenue streams, such as merchandise, touring, and other commercial licensing royalties that they would help oversee.

We were warned by many smart people that major labels—despite their excitement—were also impatient and greedy. As a new band we had little leverage to negotiate. We had heard stories from other bands and managers that if things didn't go well for Arkells in the beginning, we'd soon become an afterthought. The next band would become a priority, and all the services Atlantic was committed to providing would dissipate and we'd eventually be dropped. We were also warned that even if things went well for the band, there wouldn't be all that much money left because the label was taking a piece of all the action.

This big decision coincided with another piece of business that had previously been set aside: Joel wanted us to sign a management contract. Up to this point, he had worked with us in good faith, but now wanted to formalize an agreement. It was reasonable request, although not compulsory in the industry. Many artists have handshake deals with their managers, happily.

These were two big contracts for a young band to reckon with in the middle of a relentless touring schedule. And we had a lot of time to talk about it. Maybe too much time. We spent hours in the van driving from one town to another discussing both contracts, and I remember things becoming very blurry, very quickly. Anytime a unit spends an inordinate amount of time together, groupthink can happen. An ingroup versus out-group mentality. We developed an unhealthy sense of paranoia about our manager's intentions and Atlantic Records' motives. Too much time to think can be a curse.

What we did next is the part that I'm most embarrassed about: we put on our "business cap" and stopped being musicians. We even stopped being entrepreneurs. Entrepreneurship is fun, it's creative. We started acting more like shrewd lawyers than friends who wanted to make songs and work in the music industry as a band. We employed lawyerly tactics with bizarre principles. One line that would get repeated in our internal meetings was "If you're in no hurry, drag it out because that's when you will get the best deal." That might be true in some cases, but it's not all that true in the music business. I've learned that so much of a successful career in music is about momentum. It's about capitalizing on a moment of excitement and parlaying that capital into the next moment. Each time you do that, you have a little bit more experience and a few more friends.

This—of course—isn't to say that you should blindly sign any deal. There are countless stories of musicians who sign terrible contracts with labels and management and end up fucking themselves for years. You absolutely need to do your research and ask people smarter than you for advice. But letting things drag on is a mistake.

What ended up happening is that we spent eighteen months "negotiating" with Atlantic Records before they abruptly left the bargaining table and said goodbye. They were completely perplexed by our tactics: smiley, feel-good, and optimistic in conversation, but completely impenetrable and unmoving in contract negotiation with our lawyers. Our lawyers were confused by our instructions. It's hard to say what would've happened if we had signed with Atlantic, and there are parts of me that are curious about it. Joel—understandably—was also completely frustrated by all of this. Soon after, he threw up his hands and said see ya later. The self-inflicted chaos of our every decision only distracted us from the thing we signed up to do, which was to simply be in a band.

As we wrapped up the *Jackson Square* record cycle, we were manager-less and working with a Canadian label owned by our ex-manager who understandably hated us. We made our own plans to record our sophomore album with an esteemed American producer named Dennis Herring. The plan was to drive down to his studio in Missouri and get back to work. At the eleventh hour, our keyboard player, Dan, asked to produce the record instead. Again, *all for one and one for all*. We cancelled on Dennis.

We recorded *Michigan Left* in Canada and made new plans with our new manager, Patrick Sambrook. Upon finishing *Michigan Left*, Dan announced he was leaving the band for law school, planning to eventually join his family's practice.

We were devastated. But as we know today, a new chapter would emerge with countless lessons learned.

Looking back, I really hated so much of that time. I am embarrassed by how it was all handled. It's perfectly fine to have not signed with Atlantic, but it's inexcusable for having drawn it out that long. We only hurt our own momentum and pissed off a lot of people.

That whole episode has shaped the way I think about work ever since. I don't want to waste a lifetime negotiating. I want to have good relationships with the people closest to us, and I want to lean on their instincts. All our partners have their own businesses to run, and it's mostly an incredibly hard business. I don't assume anyone owes me their time or talent. I just hope they share an enthusiasm for the next idea that carries some potential.

The attitude you bring to any group is often as important as your skill set. Self-awareness is a valuable quality. Part of personal growth is recognizing what you're good at and where your skills are lacking. In recognizing my own short-comings when it comes to business, I've come to revere the people in my life who are guardians of my creative work—our managers, agents, accountants, and label staff. I hope they feel empowered when they're doing their jobs. I've learned that this quality—learning to delight in other people's skills—is itself a form of business acumen.

So, this is how it works now: every morning I wake up to an ongoing to-do list of *ideas*. Some are long-term projects, and some are timelier. Since there is mutual admiration with our business partners, the conversations are largely enjoyable and energizing. There are negotiations about contracts and money, but it's always with an understanding that the more we all work together and get along, the more success will be had. The inverse is also true: the less we like working together, the less successful we will be.

Developing this familiarity with the professionals around me is one of my favourite parts of the job. For example, I love our business managers and rarely question their advice. *What do I know?* I overshare so they have a clearer picture of my life. They have a keen understanding of what's important to me, and they plan accordingly. Whenever they probe me with a financial question, I reply, "Well, what would *you* do?" So far, their guidance has been instrumental in allowing me to keep my focus on creative projects.

But just to say it in print: I should confess that I am the easiest potential client for an embezzler. I would be Bernie Madoff's number one target. I'm not proud of it, but it's reached the point that I've become allergic to looking at my bank account; it only stresses me out. If I go out for dinner and I owe a friend $60 for picking up the bill, I can't even e-transfer it myself, for fear of looking at a bank statement that I don't understand. I'll email my business manager, and cc my friend, and say, "Send $60 please." So, I am writing his name—Geoff Mann—here in this book, just in case.

TEAMMATES

We've all conceived of ecosystems that help facilitate our work and creativity. Every band or group—for better or worse—develops a belief system and set of values that guides their day-to-day. It's the rhythm of communication and the division of labour between teammates that offers structure and purpose. When you're inexperienced, it's one of the only ways to provide clarity during an intense time of development. When Tim, Nick, Mike D., Dan, and I first secured ourselves as a unit, we had an artistic relationship with one another that seemed to be working. We had landed a record deal, a manager, and booking agents. We had international label executives ready to sign us. Fan by fan, we won over audiences with every show. At the time, it was impossible to imagine there were other ways to work successfully.

In 2011, when our original keyboard player, Dan, announced he was leaving the band to attend law school, it rocked our foundation. I imagine it's no different than learning a beloved colleague is leaving for another job. It was jarring, and the future became unclear. Beyond the sadness of Dan choosing to leave the band, I had genuine concerns for the first time. Well, one concern: songwriting. Songs are the nucleus of everything we do. Nothing else matters if the songs stink. All the touring, music videos, wardrobe choices, networking, gear, and literally every other part of our business means nothing if you don't have the songs. The thing that gets people to show up to the concert is the music.

Up to that point, Dan had been an influential force in our band. He had attended an arts high school and could play every instrument. For a twenty-something, he had the presence of someone much older. He was very serious about the music and obsessed over ideas of what *perfection* sounded like. His focus and experience made us all better musicians, and we learned a lot when he joined the band midway through university. Our songwriting was typical of most bands of that era. Most songs from *Jackson Square* and *Michigan Left* started with acoustic versions that I wrote, and the band would begin to jam them out in earnest, making sense of the arrangements together.

Unlike musicians who always knew they were going to make it, no one in our band necessarily expected making music to turn into an actual job. We were all realistic about how rare it was to make a career out of performing and writing music in an original band. Mike D. and Nick were ready to go to grad school. Tim was well equipped to be a gigging drummer and studio engineer. But now we had something to lose, and we didn't want to fumble it.

When Dan left the band shortly after we made *Michigan Left*, we toured the record but knew that it wouldn't be long before we had to start working on new songs again. With a member gone, we had to redevelop our working relationship. How would we manage the hole that Dan had left behind? Practically, the first thing we needed was a new keyboard player. Tim introduced Anthony to the band. They had known each other from the Mississauga punk rock scene, and we were more than confident in his abilities as a live performer. But because we had such limited experience writing with anyone outside of the band, I was doubtful we would be able to recreate the kind of songwriting chemistry we'd had up to that point. This, of course, in retrospect was incredibly naive.

Anthony offered a range of talents that were equally useful in ways we couldn't have anticipated. Not only was he a charismatic performer, but he was eager to learn and contribute to the rest of the band's operations. We shared a mutual love of The Beatles and Elton John, but he was just as interested in all the new music we were discovering in every genre. He was meticulous about his gear and put his hand up to help with all aspects of music-making and production. As he found his own lane within our team, new opportunities presented themselves for the rest of us. A new chemistry began to emerge.

In the summer of 2013, the five of us rented a room on Hughson Street North in Hamilton for $500 a month. It was a big old brick commercial building being renovated as an event space for local artists. Every other room was an active construction site, which is why the landlords were happy to earn some rent money from tenants like us who wouldn't be bothered by the noise.

The room was the opposite of acoustically treated. It was on the second floor and had big glass windows and high ceilings that only made everything that much louder. Every electric guitar chord and drum hit reverberated and bounced around the room, making it somewhat hard to hear exactly what was going on. There wasn't any air conditioning for the first few months. With the Hamilton sun beating through the big windows, shirts would come off as we worked through the tunes. None of it was physically welcoming, but it was ours.

From eleven a.m. to five p.m., five days a week, we worked on new material. For the previous two records, we had come to lean on Dan as the arbiter of many artistic decisions. With Anthony in the mix, the energy of the sessions changed. It was a bit more democratic, less intense, and we all had a bit more space to offer our opinions.

Songs started to develop quickly, and with each rehearsal we got a little tighter as a band and more comfortable with the arrangements. During those sessions we wrote "11:11," "Come To Light," "Never Thought That This Would Happen," and "Leather Jacket." We didn't have a name for the record yet, but those songs would become the *High Noon* sessions.

As our ecosystem became more collaborative, our music sounded more adventurous, even unpredictable. I came to learn that the unknown shouldn't be feared. It could be met with curiosity and an understanding that the path forward is what you make of it.

IMPOSTER SYNDROME

Occasionally, someone will come up to me and ask how I muster the courage to perform while simultaneously appearing confident and carefree. The question is often rooted in the premise that they're not good enough. They ask, "How do I get over imposter syndrome?" They are often an aspiring musician with some creative insecurity. I tell them the following: "Most people don't really give a fuck about your *journey*. I sincerely mean it. People have their own problems to worry about. They're often too busy to really be judging you. Work as hard as you can. Create something that you're proud of. Do your best. And keep it moving. Each moment is a lesson to serve the next." I don't know if this speech is perfect, and I should probably workshop it a bit more, but it's what I feel and I think it has some use.

This is not to say that I don't experience some version of imposter syndrome. I do. It's just that everyone's imposter syndrome comes out in different ways, and mine tends to reveal itself during the quiet moments off the stage when I'm left with too much time to ruminate. That's when my insecurities rise to the surface and I run into problems. When my confidence is down, it's easy to imagine all the ways I might be inadequate. In an effort to feel better and get some work done, I try to investigate the root of what's causing stress and be open to new ideas.

A case in point was when I was reading Rick Rubin's book, *The Creative Act*, which is about unlocking your creative potential. The book came out while I was writing mine, and just about every page made me feel better about my own artistic pursuits. It's a very meditative book, with short chapters that describe simple and often counterintuitive ideas about creativity.

But as much as Rubin's book was grounding and honest and felt like the truth, after sitting with it a little while, I started to have doubts. Not about the artist stuff—he nailed that on the head. It's just that the book was so good, I started to wonder whether I should even bother to write this one. "He's got everything you need in his!" I thought. But then, not many days later, I heard a clip of bestselling author Malcolm Gladwell interviewing Rubin about *The Creative Act*, and Gladwell revealed his own insecurities in relation to how he stacked up against other writers. Rubin pushed back. He said that making art is not an act of competition, it's an act of love, and therefore comparing yourself to others is beside the point. The art from two different people will be distinct, even if it's covering similar terrain. He put it plainly: Rick Rubin is the only person on planet Earth who could write a Rick Rubin book, and Malcolm Gladwell is the only person who could write a Malcolm Gladwell book. It's a very simple point, but a good one. How it compares to any other book isn't the point. The point is that it's uniquely his own, with its own voice and perspective, and that's good enough. The goal can only ever be to be the best possible version of yourself. So, I kept writing.

I've experienced this feeling while making music too. During the summer of the *High Noon* sessions, I'd head to band practice and feel overwhelmed by thoughts that our music couldn't compare to what we'd done before, let alone what else was happening in the music culture. So, it felt like fate when we got a message out of the blue in our Myspace inbox from a musical hero named Tony Hoffer.

Two years earlier, before we recorded *Michigan Left*, we had made a wish list of producers that we wanted to work with. Tony—a Los Angeles–based producer who made albums with Beck, The Kooks, M83, and Phoenix—was at the top of the list. We had reached out to his manager but heard crickets. We assumed that we weren't on his level and moved on. So, when we heard from the man himself—in a direct message on Myspace—we didn't quite understand what had happened. How had he heard of our band?

It turns out it was rather simple: Tony's manager had a new email address, and he hadn't updated it on his website.

He never got our email in the first place. This is a good lesson—don't assume just because someone doesn't get back to you that they hate you and think you're trash. That's your imposter syndrome rearing its head.

Just by chance, Tony had come across an Arkells live session online and liked what he heard. He wrote us, not having any clue that we were desperate to meet him in the first place. Two years after we'd reached out, we had a chance to head to Los Angeles and make a record with a sought-after producer.

We rented an Airbnb in Eagle Rock, a neighbourhood just outside downtown L.A., and worked six days a week in Tony's small but efficient studio. Tony expressed how competitive the music industry was, as the trends and sounds were always evolving. While he loved and owned plenty of vintage gear, he explained why it was part of his job to be open to new recording technologies. Even though he was by far the most acclaimed person we'd ever worked with, he had a sense of hustle that stayed with me. But one of the best takeaways for our band was grasping the value of working with an outside voice. Any personal quibbles that might have existed between band members didn't exist in conversations with Tony. We knew his only interest was making the songs as good as they could be.

Feeling empowered, we experimented in the studio more than ever before. We doubled Nick's bass parts with synths. We used drum machines for the first time. The songs were more heartfelt and romantic. There was no way a song with the sentimental lyrical content of "11:11" or "Dirty Blonde" would have passed the sniff test on *Jackson Square* or *Michigan Left*, but Tony gave his blessing for all those ideas and encouraged us to push even further in that direction.

Through the entire process, we developed a deeper trust and confidence in one another. When we got home in November, we were largely happy with the material, but Mike D. and Nick had a lingering sense that some of the songs could be better served. Specifically, "Cynical Bastards," "Fake Money," and "Leather Jacket." We loved all the modern and electronic touches from Tony's production style, but they were missing some of the feel that had been captured during our early jam sessions on Hughson Street in Hamilton.

So we reached out to Toronto-based rock 'n' roll heavyweight producer Eric Ratz and asked if he wanted to take a go at a few songs with us. We'd keep some parts and rerecord the stuff that wasn't sitting right. Unlike Tony, who usually listened back to the songs at a moderate volume, Eric loved to turn the studio monitors up to eleven and feel the power of the drums and bass. Once we had a song in a good place, he'd say, "It's time for a glory listen!" and we'd let the songs wash over us as if they were pumping through arena speakers. We were low on time and money, but Eric put the finishing touches on those songs, and our record was complete. Mike's and Nick's instincts were entirely correct.

At first glance, Tony Hoffer and Eric Ratz couldn't be more different. Tony is five-foot-seven, slim, with a crisp haircut and thick-rimmed glasses. Eric is six-foot-three with long blond hair, and lumbers around like a football player wearing a Sabbath shirt. Their workflow and energy in the room are totally different. But they're both uniquely gifted in their own ways. They have taught me that a successful creative process can look and feel different at various stages, while still enjoying it all the same.

The validation for this new process came shortly after *High Noon* was released. As we began to tour that record, we realized that our biggest songs in the set were now from that album. The reaction to "Leather Jacket" continues to be one of the biggest moments of an Arkells show. It's a song that's been covered in pubs all over the world. It's a song that drunk dudes at sporting events start singing to me as I pass them in the beer line. I am grateful for that song.

Today, I work at a pace that doesn't allow much room for imposter syndrome. It never goes away completely, no matter how much success you have, and I can always feel it coming on when we have too much free time. Continuing to work and evolve is the ultimate antidote. Lucky for me, that pursuit is never-ending. Accepting that you will never have all the answers because the goal-posts keep moving shouldn't scare you. It should liberate you. I will add this to my "People don't give a fuck about your journey" pep talk. Second-guessing is a healthy part of creation, but questioning your own self-worth is not.

PROJECT MANAGER

Developing a sense of confidence in your work and career doesn't mean you're always right. In a collaborative job, it's a constant dance of including and empowering your partners while understanding that not every collaboration is the right fit. Relationships can run their course. But when conflict arises, it's important to ask yourself if you're the problem. And to be genuinely curious about it.

In 2015, I was *really* beginning to wonder if we were the problem. We had just released our third record, *High Noon*, and had the unfortunate distinction of already having worked with three different managers. A band's relationship with their manager is usually taken as seriously as a marriage, and we were considering our third divorce. It was an odd predicament for us, because I otherwise got on great with everyone in our extended team. I enjoyed the relationships with all our other partners, admiring our producers, booking agents, publicists, and label team. But the most important relationship—our management team, the position responsible for interacting with all arms of our business—never quite settled in.

There are many arms in the music business, but an artist's manager is the control centre for their career. Like many small business operations, the job can be a bit nebulous, as there are no limits to what a good manager might want to take on. But like any other organization, you need good leadership at the top. A good manager will whip everyone into shape. They are responsible for jockeying for time and attention from your partners, who work with a roster of other acts, and their own network of professional relationships. If your manager is unorganized and your goals aren't communicated clearly to your partners, it's hard to get much done. It's a big job, and managers have to wear a lot of hats. A manager must understand not only the uneven daily rhythms of an artist but also the nuances of, say, a tour offer. To manage a band like ours, you must be a high-level communicator, part-time psychologist, HR person, and top-level administrator.

In the music business, if an artist is rolling through managers at our rate, it's likely a red flag. It's that old expression: "If you run into an asshole in the morning, you ran into an asshole. If you run into assholes all day, you're the asshole." Were *we* the asshole?

Looking back on how we parted ways with our manager Joel, our band had developed an unhealthy "us against the world" attitude, and "the world" included our management.

We were headstrong, indecisive, and utterly confusing to Joel. This led to a growing distrust between both parties, and communication became trying on both sides. There are many things I would've done much differently, but operating from a place of trust is where I'd start. If trust dissipates, then there isn't much of a relationship. There had been a sizable personality conflict, and I did little to keep the peace.

Before our second record, *Michigan Left*, we hired Patrick, a smart and warm guy with good instincts who had experience handling many successful artists, including The Tragically Hip. He carved out a new record deal with Universal Music and secured us the opening spot on The Hip's national tour in 2013. Nevertheless, as the album cycle wound down, I couldn't help but feel we weren't putting enough energy and resources into building the band internationally, and I felt like my enterprising attitude and never-ending list of international marketing ideas were becoming mostly a pain in the ass. Inevitably, we went our separate ways. Patty was gracious about it, but there were days when I wondered if maybe I just wanted too much. After all, we owed Patty a lot for getting our band on track.

We figured the best path forward was to work with someone who'd be directly interacting with the international music business every day. Our next stop was with an American-based manager named Tom Sarig, a larger-than-life figure from New York City whose roster included Lou Reed and bands we loved, like The Gaslight Anthem.

Tom was a dynamic personality, *if* you could get ahold of him. Like many people in our business, he was an excellent name-dropper, and it always felt as if we were inches away from a new record deal, opening a hot tour, or landing press in *Rolling Stone*. He absolutely had the right relationships, but I never felt like he was able to leverage them to our benefit.

We were beginning to get itchy feet again, but I was very attuned to how ditching yet another manager might make us look—especially to prospective managers. At that point we desperately needed someone in our corner who would go the extra mile. It was a calculation any professional must consider at one point or another: stick with the status quo or believe there might be a better fit out there. So, while we were on tour in the U.K., I called our long-time entertainment lawyer Chris Taylor to have a conversation we'd already had three times before: "I think we need a new manager. What should we do?"

When seeking advice, find the person in your life who's best equipped to answer the question at hand. In our case, we needed someone with a bird's-eye view of our situation in the greater industry landscape. Seeking counsel solely from an artist friend who'd happily get worked up and pissed off on our behalf would have been unhelpful. We needed to find a person with the right knowledge and experience who could see both sides. Chris was an industry veteran who could offer sober-minded and even-handed insight into our situation.

As I walked around the streets of Brighton on the phone, I asked Chris if *we* were the problem. Had we become *that band*? The delusional and difficult band the industry is quietly whispering about. Chris listened as I explained how Tom wasn't the kind of active manager that I felt we needed in that moment. I worried that he wasn't looking far enough beyond our growing Canadian business and pushing things further internationally.

Chris was always a great listener and calming presence for our band. He's had a remarkable journey in music. After solidifying a career in entertainment law, he launched Last Gang Records and Management, which helped discover and invest in the early careers of bands like Metric and Death From Above 1979. As a lawyer, he was responsible for brokering U.S. record deals for some of Canada's biggest exports like Sum 41, Nelly Furtado, and Drake.

As a fellow scrapper with endless energy, Chris understood our situation better than anyone. He assured me that we weren't the problem; we just hadn't found the right fit yet. This insight was reassuring. Chris had belief in the character, talent, and work ethic of our band. Even though we had been through three managers, it was, all things considered, a relatively small sample size. If you're looking to get married, sometimes you have to date a few people before you find the right long-term fit.

Finally, I said, "Chris, I enjoy talking to you about all this stuff. Can *you* just manage us please?" I could hear Chris's voice lighten up a little bit as he explained, to my surprise, that after a hiatus from music management he was re-entering that part of the business. He had begun to work with a talented young manager named Ashley Poitevin, with whom he co-managed the electro-pop artist Lights. Ashley (or Ash as we now affectionately call her) was our age, and we'd become friendly at music industry events over the years. An arrangement with Chris and Ash seemed to offer the best of both worlds: we'd have internationally respected management and the comfort and familiarity of home.

What we didn't know at the time was that Ash was the burst of life that our band needed. At first, Ash acted as a dutiful day-to-day manager, responsible for understanding our business and helping to coordinate our calendar. But the more we worked together, the more I began to realize that she was *much more* than that. In her smiley upbeat way, I eventually learned that she was a *killer*, seeing every angle and anticipating every move.

Once we started working together, things began to click. From our partners, I could immediately sense a respect for our new managers and excitement to work alongside them because they were invested in all the right ways. Communication flowed effortlessly between all parties. They knew our history, our style of work, and what we wanted to do next.

In the fall of 2016, we played two sold-out shows at Massey Hall, the legendary "bucket list" theatre in Toronto. We sold around five thousand tickets, which was far more than we could ever have hoped for. I don't think we ever really thought about where we might play *after* Massey Hall, but Ash was already plotting.

Shortly after, she suggested our next Toronto show should be at Budweiser Stage the following summer. Budweiser Stage holds . . . sixteen thousand people. That's more than three times as many tickets as we had sold for our shows at Massey Hall. The band was amused by this idea but completely apprehensive about the prospect of taking on such an ambitious show. How would we sell all those tickets? What would an Arkells show on that scale even look like? It's one thing to conceive of a stage design with appropriate lighting and production flourishes for a club or a theatre, but an amphitheatre where the biggest acts in the world play was uncharted territory for us at the time. The scope of it all seemed unimaginable, but Ash believed in our ability to pull it off. It's one thing to be a big dreamer; it's another to be prepared to do the mountain of work that comes with ambitious ideas. Ash turned out to especially revel in the second part. She was able to identify and articulate the qualities that made us stand out. Ash had been a fan of Arkells since our first record, and she recognized that even in small clubs the show itself always felt big. She saw things in us that we couldn't yet see in ourselves. We talked it over and agreed that if we could get to ten thousand tickets, it would be a huge win. Nobody expected the show to sell out. But it did. And quickly too.

Every artist should seek out this kind of collaborator—one with the right combination of instinct, personal taste, and trust. One by one, Ash can go through each member of Arkells and describe how we best shine, and then she gently nudges us in that direction. A good manager understands your ambitions and fights for you. In a competitive field, you hope your manager has enough cachet to manufacture new opportunities and can negotiate the best deals on your behalf. A *great* manager will see things in you and believe in your abilities in ways that even you don't fully understand. The intimacy of the relationship is why it's so important. If there is a clash in principles, taste, or work ethic, an artist might be leaving something on the table. A band has only one career, which is why you must try and get it right.

There are many stories in rock 'n' roll lore that document some crooked manager who embezzled money or took advantage of an artist, but our career doesn't have any of that. Our story contains several softer, subtler lessons. I learned plenty from each manager, and all offered lessons in how to build a successful enterprise. They were qualified and skilled, but those relationships also uncovered what was still missing from the equation. Beyond unrelenting work ethic, strategic planning, and strong communications skills, someone who offered optimism and light and had reverence for the work was something that turned out to be important to me. In a job where you need to show bursts of life with every new song and performance, I needed someone who kept the job fun and youthful.

The best thing about working with someone who has such boundless passion? It is contagious. Ash leads by example. She greets every idea with some wonder and curiosity and is energized by the process itself. A group must have an "all for one" quality to survive, and that is the root of Ash's management style. When you see a leader whose intentions are only centred on the health and success of the team, negative instincts that often permeate group work begin to evaporate. She is by far the biggest fan of Arkells, and it's not even close. She is attentive to the needs of every band member, making sure we're comfortable and that we're heard. She is charmed by the best parts of what we do, but I can always tell when she thinks something sucks. We don't agree on everything, but we agree on *almost* everything.

For me, I've found the person who can keep up with my scattered brain *and* my ambition to keep evolving. She helps make sense of new ideas and can tell me if they're good or a waste of time. She is fiercely loyal and quietly protects us from the many stressful parts of the job. She treats Arkells fans, the crew, and our partners with the respect and courtesy they deserve. And she will kill anyone who fucks with us. And that's why we will never have to fire another manager.

SONGWRITING

When I sit at the piano to work on a new song now, I'm often doing roughly the same thing I did when I was fifteen years old. The piano keys are laid out in a very simple way: they go left to right in a straight line, low to high. At a piano, I can replicate an entire band at once. My head bops, imagining a beat the drums might play. The notes played by my left hand will replicate the bass guitar, often stabbing a single low note. With my right hand, I'll use my thumb, middle, and pinky fingers to form a chord, and this will act as a rhythm guitar. I can sing the melody a lead guitar or synth might play. Guitars, their strings and frets, are inherently more complicated to me, and as a result I feel less free playing one. Piano—the way I see it and play it—is more liberating and feels like something any novice could handle. I still feel like a novice when I play.

I don't need to write every day. I often write when something is stirring inside of me. I am looking for a very specific alchemy between the chords, melody, and words. All three things are contextual to each other. If some simple chords (say, C major to F major) are accompanied by the wrong combination of melody or words, it will feel pedestrian and predictable. Sometimes, those same chords with another set of words and melody can feel profound. Sometimes it's the sound of the instrument that influences where the melody goes. A piano, guitar, or synth all evoke something different and can steer a song in any number of directions.

So much of my day-to-day life informs my lyrics. Our song "Tragic Flaw," for instance, which I wrote when I was sixteen, was inspired by one of my English classes. I can't remember exactly, but I bet we were reading Shakespeare and I decided to start playing with the literary term for a character's shortcoming that leads to their ultimate downfall. Our song "Abigail," also from our first album, *Jackson Square*, is a love story that takes place in a food court between Abigail and Zach. The concept came from Ben Folds's song "Zak and Sara," a drama of sorts, about two kids in love hanging out in a guitar store.

I often find myself lifting directly from friends and funny things they've said. The song "John Lennon," from *Jackson Square*, is about a classmate I had a crush on. She wanted to author an autobiography, which I found amusing given her relatively short and charming life. I was explaining the situation to Nick as we walked around McMaster one night, and he quipped, "She should get Frank McCourt to write the forward to her book." He was referring to the author Frank McCourt who wrote a memoir called *Angela's Ashes* about his painful, poverty-stricken upbringing in 1930s Ireland. I thought that line was so fucking funny, and it made it into the song.

When writing a song, there are moments when you get inevitably stuck, unsure if each section—the verse, pre-chorus, and chorus—are interacting as they should. You wonder if you're making the most musically compelling choice, or if the lyrics are naturally rolling off your tongue just right. It's hard to know what the "correct" answer is, but you can feel it in your body when it's not working. And that's why living with a song that you *know* has potential is such a physically immersive feeling. You feel it inside of you, rumbling in your stomach. You have the words and chords and an inkling that there might be some gold in there, so you have no choice but to keep digging. You keep clearing the clutter of clunky ideas until you find something that feels clean and precise and best represents the emotion you're trying to convey. Even if you're making a song about a dream world, you want it to feel real and honest. Sometimes that can come in three minutes; sometimes it can take months. And I know better now than to assume there is any one path to discovering an idea, let alone finishing one.

THE SHOW

Whenever I go to a concert, it inevitably turns into a work trip. Occasionally I allow myself to get swept away by the performance, but most of the time I can't help but try to figure out what worked about the show—and what was missing.

If you want your own art to get better, the first step is observing how other artists do it. As a live performer, I want to know how the greats leave a lasting impression on their audiences. Once the show is over, the final part of my research is noting the mood of the fans as they *exit* the venue. You can always feel the hum of a crowd after a great show. I imagine asking strangers what parts of the show they enjoyed the most. My guess is they'd give a version of the same response: they're happy they heard the hits, the band seemed *really* into it, and a few unexpected moments made the night feel like something that couldn't be repeated.

When I was nine years old, I went to a production of *Joseph and the Amazing Technicolor Dreamcoat*, starring Donny Osmond. There was a moment at the end of the show when he floated through the theatre, held by a harness. As he got higher, he waved to those of us sitting in the upper balcony, and I was certain we locked eyes for a moment and he smiled at me. That's my entire memory of the show. I bet if you were to ask people all the things they liked about a show a few weeks after it, most would be hard-pressed to identify the specific details that stood out. They would, however, remember the *feeling* it left them with. The feeling is the thing that lasts.

Creating a performance that gives a lasting feeling is often the result of many complicated artistic and production choices but is grounded in a very simple concept: preparation. Learning from the greats is learning to be prepared, and to handle even the smallest decisions with the care and thought you would the big ones. A great show is the sum of its parts.

In 2012, I saw Bruce Springsteen play at the Rogers Centre—the stadium where the Toronto Blue Jays play. This was my second time seeing Springsteen, and I went with a group of diehard Boss fans who take the ritual very seriously. Despite having seen over three hundred Springsteen shows, our one friend's excitement was reminiscent of a giddy fourth grader at a sleepover, and his reverence rivalled that of a religious zealot. He insisted we line up outside the stadium at three p.m. so we could be at the front of the barricade.

Watching him reminded me that people come to a concert to get swept away by the magic of it all, and most aren't taking in a show with an analytical lens.

At eight p.m., Bruce took the stage in front of a packed house and held forty thousand people in the palm of his hand for almost four hours. The show has stayed with me since. It was a masterclass in preparation, and I left with many little lessons about how to put on a good show. But most importantly I came away with a *philosophy*. I realized that the success of a show that hopes to leave a fan with a lasting feeling is the result of a hundred little creative choices strung together, each of which matters just as much as the next.

Bruce's attention to the audience's experience was demonstrated from the first note. To start, Springsteen and his band entered the stage as the house speakers blasted an organ version of "Take Me Out to the Ball Game"—a nod to the baseball stadium we were standing in. I chuckled. Immediately, drummer Max Weinberg started the beat, not allowing for any awkward silence. This is a small detail, but a welcome change from the indie rock scene, where bands often clumsily tune their guitars for the first forty-five seconds of the show, completely killing any buzz generated by their arrival on stage. Bruce strutted to the front of the catwalk and started strumming his guitar, shaking his hips like Elvis, and opened with the song "Working on the Highway" from *Born in the U.S.A.* He looked up at the crowd and in a charming American twang hollered, with a smile, "Let me take a look at you!" pointing and waving to the fans in the upper deck.

In the first twenty-five seconds of the show, I learned three lessons that we've applied to every performance since:

1. Show up equipped with a thoughtful walk-on moment.
2. Capitalize on the energy of the show; do not allow for any awkward pauses.
3. Give some love to the crowd in the back.

Beyond that, Bruce was heartfelt and emotional and funny—sometimes all at once—and I could point to countless other moments throughout the night that lifted the entire crowd. It was clear Bruce had a bag of tricks that he'd been adding to for over forty years. Depending on the mood of the night and what he determined the audience needed, he expertly guided the show through a series of scripted and unscripted moments. Like any great touring musician, he is a student of performance.

None of what Bruce did was rocket science. And he surely didn't invent the tricks himself; he borrowed from his heroes and then made each one his own. He had clearly imagined how each moment might feel for the crowd and came up with a plan to optimize and wring every drop out of those feelings. If you create these moments, you grow your relationship with your audience. After that night, "Working on the Highway"—the tune he opened with and one I barely knew—became one of my favourites, and I left an even bigger fan.

When you are comfortable on stage, every curveball becomes a little easier to handle. An inexperienced artist might get thrown off by a guitar string breaking or a piece of equipment malfunctioning, but a professional can roll with the punches. Like a skilled stand-up comedian dealing with a rowdy crowd, Springsteen seemed to be hunting for unscripted, improvised moments. At his show, I learned the power of spontaneity. Homemade signs with song requests are customary for fans at Springsteen shows, and given his extensive catalogue, the signs in the crowd usually feature some deep cuts. Throughout the show, I watched as Bruce scanned the audience, contemplating his next trick. While the E Street Band jammed the final outro of one song, he'd grab a fan sign, hold it up for his band to see, and then cue the audible. The song on the sign was not on the setlist. On a dime, the big band would launch into the request, and nobody missed a beat. The whole thing was *seamless*. But what I quickly realized was that the spontaneity of the moment was an act of preparation itself. It couldn't have happened if the band wasn't a well-oiled machine, ready to play any of Springsteen's hundreds of songs.

That concert crystalized concepts that I already innately understood but was still developing the language and awareness to articulate. When you're trying to entertain, the audience shouldn't need an academic understanding of what you're doing; they should just be entertained! They don't need to know the inner workings of how a moment came together or *why* a moment is clever or impactful. They just need to feel it. But as the performer, it's a puzzle that needs to be put together, and it's easier to complete if you have a vision of what you're trying to create.

Like most things, the best way to improve is through experience. Through trial and error from hundreds of shows. When I stop to think about it, I realize I've been developing my own bag of tricks for years and have been building my own tool set. But experience itself is only part of the equation. The other part is the conscious reflection on each show—attempt to recognize what worked and what didn't, and then harness the next opportunity for magic that might arise when you're onstage. From the first time I ever played for a crowd, there were valuable lessons I was learning—often by happenstance.

In grade 11, with a couple shows under our belt, my high school band, The Lizzies, signed up for a battle of the bands on Church Street in Toronto. We'd prepared our set with newly written songs, and I worked hard selling tickets to everyone in my school. When the day came, we loaded our gear into the venue and anxiously waited for our time to play. I had high hopes for the show and envisioned the lasting impression we'd leave on the crowd; this was surely going to be the beginning of *something special*. We took the stage, and problems began straightaway. I realized we had forgotten to tune our instruments. Nothing sounded right, and the entire set was a disaster. A rudimentary note, but it can't be overstated: for a seamless performance, your equipment ought to work. I tell any musician who plans to play live that the first piece of gear they should buy is a tuning pedal. First things first!

Later that year, we performed a two-song set at the North Toronto Collegiate talent show, playing a cover of Weezer's "Undone (The Sweater Song)," before launching into Coldplay's "Yellow." Even though it took place under the florescent lighting of the school's cafeteria and with no formal stage, I suggested to the band that we all wear knit sweaters for the first song (get it?) only to execute a wardrobe change to reveal yellow T-shirts underneath (get it?!). The crowd was amused, and it strengthened the overall performance. In a two-song set, I was already learning the value of a gag and the power of wardrobe choices.

During the second song, I grasped the importance of having a sense of humour and keeping cool under pressure. My guitar strap came off halfway through the first verse of "Yellow," and I was left unsure what to do as the band played on. Instead of singing Chris Martin's lyrics, I improvised new ones: "My guitar strap, yes, my guitar strap has fallllllllll-len off my shoulder." Alex, our lead guitarist, came to the rescue by reattaching the strap, while the band and crowd shared a laugh, and we were back on track by the time we hit the chorus. This, of course, illustrated a disregard for the first rule—our equipment was not working—but it illuminated an equally important skill: improvisation. These days, I still try to embrace the situation when something breaks on stage. Our crew frantically runs around trying to fix the problem, and when they inevitably do, we celebrate them like they just won a boxing match, and the crowd goes nuts. Like Springsteen, I try to greet every spontaneous moment with a grin.

I, of course, didn't know all the lessons I was learning during these formative performances, but they stuck with me. In those early years, it was all gut instinct and there wasn't much planning beyond rehearsing the music itself, but now I understand what I have always been searching for: I am looking to create moments of connection. Moments of surprise, joy, and community. It's the feeling that I chase and prepare for at every Arkells show, and it's the thing that you love about your favourite performers too.

When you graduate to bigger rooms, the assignment evolves, but the fundamentals of the show remain the same. With time, Arkells have developed a strong work ethic that simply builds on the lessons from every show. We're constantly evaluating what's working and what's not. When we rehearse for a tour, we don't spend much time rehearsing the songs themselves, but instead think about the moments *within* the songs and how we best transition from one to the next. What will the breakdown in the bridge sound like? When will I address the crowd and tell a story? How do we create layers to the performance? There is an electric current throughout each concert that we try our best to attune to— we know it's our job to lead the dance.

VINCE_KERMAN

In grade 7, Ms. Janes assigned the class a research project. Each student was asked to interview someone in the community that had a job we might want one day and then write about what we learned.

Most of my classmates reached out to their parents' friends—dental hygienists or mechanics—while others went over to the local fire station and spoke to a firefighter. Those approaches didn't feel particularly interesting to me. It was 1999, and I had a singular focus in my life. I was obsessed with Vince Carter, the new star of the Toronto Raptors, and I wondered if I could somehow use the assignment to get closer to Vince.

My newly minted email address was vince_kerman@hotmail.com. I invited Vince to my birthday party (he did not reply), attended his basketball camp in the summer, and drew pictures of him during art class. Knowing I probably wouldn't hear back from the man himself, I took a different track. I decided to get in touch with the person who'd drafted Vince. The person responsible for this decision was the Raptors general manager, Glen Grunwald. Glen, a former Division 1 college basketball player turned lawyer turned sports executive, was the architect of the team. It was an ambitious idea but also potentially a very fun one.

I opened the phone book and flipped to the back where the businesses were listed. I found the number for the Toronto Raptors front office and their address at the recently opened Air Canada Centre. Without wasting a moment, I called and the receptionist answered.

In my twelve-year-old preteen voice, I nervously asked, "Can I please speak to Mr. Glen Grunwald?"

"Please hold."

Within a minute, I was put through to his secretary. With my heart pounding, I explained in my most professional tone the nature of the school assignment and how Glen had my dream job. Maybe it was the randomness of my request or perhaps the fact that I'd caught her off guard, but she agreed to arrange a phone call with Glen. Immediately, my school assignment became the most fun and exciting thing in my life. The instinct to find an adventure in any potentially mundane assignment was revealing: chasing the thing that's reasonable and obvious will never have quite the same payoff as chasing the thing that *really* excites you.

I called Glen while he was on the road with the team in Charlotte, North Carolina. We spoke for twenty minutes, and he was very patient and kind with my questions. I emailed him some follow-up questions the next week. For my birthday, through some secret coordination with my dad, he gave me a backstage tour of the arena and dressing room before a Raptors game.

Throughout the entire experience, I was so genuinely thrilled to have a relationship with Glen. I felt incredibly lucky. The rush of calling his office. The emails back and forth. It was purely so much fun. It's a feeling that has since become a part of my daily life and work.

I'm not sure where the instinct to *ask* comes from, but why not? If you get in the habit of reaching out and connecting dots, and it becomes a part of your life, the stakes are never particularly high. I'm just poking around and seeing what might happen. I don't feel like anyone owes me anything; I simply hope that someone sees a spark of something fun or interesting or of mutual benefit. Or simple kindness. You should assume you will rarely get the response you're looking for, but that's okay. If you hold grudges and have the memory of an elephant, you might feel betrayed or resentful. Luckily, I have the memory of a goldfish.

KINDRED SPIRITS

Because so many of my interests and passions exist within my job, it's often hard to turn off. Even though my life is centred on my passion, it's important to have moments of space. Moments away from work to play can reinvigorate my process. I've observed the importance of this not only with artists but with anyone whose job is all-encompassing.

For me, it's hoops. Basketball is purely playtime. Exercise provides physical release. It gets me away from my brain and into my body and somehow improves my mental sharpness in the process. When I'm on the basketball court, it feels like I'm opening up new mental pathways for everyday problem-solving. Researchers can give you the science behind it, but I'm here to tell ya it works! If the weather is good, I start most of our North American tours by buying a fresh basketball and finding a public court to shoot around in the day. It's a great way to connect with a new place and have an interaction with strangers from different worlds.

Even if I'm not on the court, watching a good basketball game is immersive enough to pull me away from all of my musical preoccupations, or at least allow my brain to work on them in the background. In the spring of 2019, I went to several NBA playoff games to watch my Toronto Raptors battle through each round and spent the rest of them in sports bars with all my friends. With every game, we lost our minds, experiencing pain and joy and everything in between. The team was incredibly likeable, led by a first-year head coach named Nick Nurse and a veteran squad who were there to get the job done. The most legendary moment in Canadian basketball history occurred during Game 6 of the Eastern Conference semifinal, when Kawhi Leonard hit "The Shot" at the buzzer to send the team to the next round. You know it—Kawhi shoots a fade-away jumper in the corner, falling to the ground, as an arena watched the ball bounce around the rim a bunch of times before it finally dropped through the hoop to send the team to the conference final. I was at the game and freaked out like I had just won a twenty-million-dollar lottery, hugging every stranger around me. The clip of my childlike giddy enthusiasm ended up in most sports highlights recaps that weekend and beyond.

As it turned out, I had a flight to Los Angeles the next morning to do some songwriting. Wearing my Raptors T-shirt from the night prior, I landed in L.A. at eleven a.m. and quickly dropped my suitcase at the house our label rented to artists and called an Uber. As I waited, I sat at the out-of-tune grand piano in the living room and started singing a phrase that had been running through my mind on the plane ride. Reflecting on the newfound luck of a Toronto sports fan, I started humming "years in the making" over some sentimental chords. It had been twenty-six years since a Toronto team had any real shot at a championship.

I made a little voice note and headed across town for the session. When I got there, I explained to the producer my obsession with the Raptors and how I'd been at the historic game the night before. I played the demo recording and felt sort of embarrassed about a song that was kind of about a *basketball game*. But it was a place to start, capturing an authentic feeling, and we got to work on it. I left that afternoon with the start of a new Arkells song. Little did I know, I was in the midst of a *new* run-in with the Raptors.

Earlier in the season, my friend Adam Burchill, who worked with Maple Leafs Sports and Entertainment, the parent company of the Raptors, had reached out to me with an odd request: Nick Nurse was looking for an electric piano for his office. Adam is a mensch and knew that this would be exactly the kind of thing we'd like to help with, and Arkells found him a piano.

As the playoffs rolled on, a funny thing began to happen. The country watched head coach Nick Nurse lead the Raptors through the playoffs, and it seemed every time he was seen getting off the team plane or walking through the tunnel in the arena, he'd have a guitar gig bag over his shoulder. *What was with this coach who looked like he was about to head to an open mic night?* The behaviour was somewhat unprecedented in the world of professional sports. During press conferences Nick explained that he was a new musician, and not only did playing help him relax, he believed that it unlocked a kind of creativity that helped him as a coach. For Raptors fans it was all part of the magic. The Raptors went on to beat the Golden State Warriors in the final to capture the NBA title, and our new unreleased song "Years In The Making" made even more sense to me.

As we basked in the glory of the Raptors win, I had a thought: Arkells had a sold-out show at Budweiser Stage coming up on Saturday June 22, nine days after the Raptors had won the championship. So, I tried the same thing I had done twenty years earlier: I called the Raptors front office. Well, emailed. I was put in touch with Nick's chief of staff, Geni, and asked if Nick would be interested in joining us onstage during the set and performing "Signed, Sealed, Delivered (I'm Yours)" by Stevie Wonder. The right song for the moment. My expectations were roughly the same as when I'd called the Raptors front office two decades prior. A fun idea, but a slim chance. To our surprise, Geni replied and said Nick would be happy to join the band.

On the day of the show, Nick arrived at soundcheck to run the song, and we met in person for the first time. I hadn't mentioned the idea to our extended band or crew, and the look on everyone's face was total surprise and sheer excitement. Nick explained to me that he'd never played in front of a crowd before and was quite nervous. I gave him my guitar, put my arm around his shoulder, and promised him that he had nothing to worry about. I told him to look around at the extended powerhouse band he'd be playing with: a six-piece horn section and three backup singers.

"Just enjoy it! And if you get lost, stick to the E chord. The song is in E. You can't fuck it up."

It was a perfect summer night without a cloud in the sky. From the first song, the whole place was alive and dancing. Halfway though, I addressed the crowd: "We have a special guest for the next song. You've seen him. Everywhere he goes, he has a guitar on his shoulder. Let's give it up for Canada's hottest guitarist: the head coach of your championship-winning Toronto Raptors, Nick Nurse!"

Nick walked onstage, and it felt like sixteen thousand heads exploded. People had been drunk on the Raptors for the last three months and this put them on another planet. We launched into the song, featured Nick at the end of the cat-walk during the bridge, and ended the performance with big guitar hits around Tim's drum kit riser. It couldn't have gone better. After the show, Nick told me that he was more nervous for the performance than for Game 6 of the final. "Coaching in the final, no problem! Playing guitar in front of sixteen thousand people? I don't know how you do it!"

Getting to know Nick since, I am constantly reminded of the value of leading with passion and curiosity. He devours books not only about coaching and leadership but about music and creativity. There's no limit to his imagination, and his outlets outside his job have added to his routine and success. Anyone who's made it as far as Nick has a baseline obsession with their work, but after that, it's a matter of finding complementary outlets to run alongside that drive. We're all in search of some equilibrium, and that's what music does for Nick, and what sports does for me.

Throughout his career, Nick has relentlessly pursued the *next adventure*, unafraid to swing big, take chances, and carve out his own path. After playing in college, he started at the very bottom of the basketball world, player coaching in the British Basketball League, before slowly grinding for the next twenty-five years on his way to an NBA head coaching job. Each coaching stint was a stepping stone to the next— building a body of knowledge, a work ethic, and lifelong relationships.

The best part about finding new creative outlets is that you don't know where they might lead. The twelve-year-old basketball fan in me could never have predicted that a Raptors head coach would text me cover songs he had recorded from his hotel room. But that's exactly what he does. When he's on the road, Nick takes on everything from Prince to Elton John and even Arkells. He has a raspy voice from all his side-line screaming and a Midwestern twang that reminds me of Bob Dylan. One day we'll release our Nurse/Kerman co-write called "On a Plane About to Land in Houston."

STAYING POWER

After starting the band with Mike D. and Nick, our first paying gig came in at $80, gross. We didn't learn the difference between net and gross income until years later, and if you were to ask Nick, he'd argue I still don't really understand. Either way, $80 felt like a lot of money, especially for something I would've *paid* to do.

So, every time we made a dollar, we put it away for a time when we were in need of gas money to get to the next gig or book some studio recording time. We only ever conceived of the band's earnings as a tool for investing in the next show or the next song. This is still part of our philosophy today.

The first two shows we played were unpaid, so there wasn't anything to invest: we won our campus battle of the bands before placing second in the Ontario-wide final. From there, we were ready for our next step. The goal was very specific. It was landing a gig at the Casbah, a hallowed venue in downtown Hamilton.

With a low ceiling and shallow stage, the Casbah might break the fire code with more than 150 people, but it never felt small to us. It was *important*. During our first year of school, we'd leave the lush McMaster University campus and take the city bus downtown to watch many of the great Canadian indie rock bands perform there. Inside those sweaty four walls, we learned so much from acts like The Weakerthans, Constantines, Stars, and Joel Plaskett.

Brodie Schwendiman was the venue's promoter, and I figured I should muster some courage and introduce myself. One night as I approached the club for a show, I saw Brodie heading in the same direction. I shuffled up to him and asked, "Excuse me, sir—are you Brodie?"

He looked at me suspiciously. "Ya, why?"

"I just wanted to say thank you for the amazing shows at your club. It's the best." As his face lightened, he thanked me, and a friendship developed.

Brodie connected us with a local Hamilton band called Frantic City and asked if we wanted to open their next headlining show. We jumped at the chance. I don't remember a ton about the show, except that it was a busy room and I was pleased that we'd done it. As the bar was closing up, the lead singer came by, thanked us for being on the bill, and reassured us that we'd be compensated. I answered with genuine surprise: "Really? Sure, whatever! Thank you!"

A few weeks later he came by our residence and dropped off our pay for the evening: eighty bucks. Split between a band, there aren't many figures that could be less than $80, but somehow it was far more money than I'd been expecting. Artists should be compensated for their work, but we knew that if we wanted to play our own songs and make our own name, we'd have to *earn* it.

Playing in a band is a precarious job, and even when we were starting out, we were realistic about our future. There are so many things that need to click, and continue to be nurtured, for a band to stay together. Most groups, if they're lucky, have a window of a few years when they creatively shine together and find an audience. In the sea of new music, not to mention the countless artists that came before, every artist is a drop of water in an ocean. If you *do* have fans, it becomes a matter of not only holding on to them but also trying to make new ones. It requires a consistent output of new music and regular touring to keep the collective interest alive. Beyond those external factors, there are countless internal factors that can sabotage your potential: Does the group have chemistry and respect for one another? Do they like each enough to soldier on down unknown roads? The one thing that has the power to sabotage everything? Money.

We're lucky that our band was aligned on our music and work ethic early on, and even luckier that we were able to align on investing in ourselves as a guiding idea. There has been an unspoken understanding that the art and shows must be served first, and we will pay ourselves later. From the beginning, we innately believed that if we wanted people to keep showing up, we had to be consistently good, and that meant putting the money right back into the band. I often think about the great creatives who stop at nothing to see their projects through, revering and respecting the work every step of the way. This is what I aspire to do. I want to be proud of everything we make, knowing we didn't cut corners.

Of course, I was born with countless privileges that have allowed me to adopt this attitude about both money and opportunity. The unearned confidence that comes with checking every box of societal good fortune is something I'm very aware of. And my mother is too. When I finished school, I asked if I could move home to save money, and she laughed, only offering a terse "Absolutely not." And that was the end of the conversation. Rent, and life, was now up to me to sort out, and the expectation was that I'd develop a scrappy attitude, quickly.

Any healthy aspect of our relationship with money started with our first bookkeeper, Nick. Nick's dad was an accountant, and they both helped the band organize our finances. On the road, Nick was responsible for settling with the promoter at the end of the night and holding onto the money. For the first number of years, Nick would closely guard a yellow pencil case containing cash and receipts. If the sum exceeded $500, we'd pull into some parking lot with a bank machine on our way to the hotel after a show—usually around one a.m.—and Nick would dutifully put the money in our account. It became part of our routine on tour.

As we were coming up, we heard stories from friends in bands warning us that even if we were starting to make money, it wouldn't last very long. To provide structure and consistency, our accountant Geoff put us on modest quarterly payouts and squirrelled the rest away. Having worked with musicians for decades, he had a more holistic understanding of the business than we did.

It might seem like an obvious point, but longevity comes from *continuing to work*. There's a lot that goes into continuing to work, but so much of it comes down to money—not just how much of it there is, but how everyone feels about it. In our collaboration, we want to keep the creative plans at the centre of what we do. One of the reasons we've been able to keep our focus on the art is because we split the money five ways. All the songwriting royalties, merch revenue, live performance guarantees, and everything else goes into the pot. It's allowed us to write more songs, create more freely, and plan for the future because everyone's financial stake has been the same.

Above all, one of the most important lessons I've continued to learn and relearn is that with any entrepreneurial pursuit, *you get to make up the rules*. And the rules can evolve. Everything we do is contextual to the place, time, and circumstances. The way we approached our debut record was different than our third record and different than our eighth record. And each investment was specific to the goals we had in the moment.

Maybe I sound like a savvy business operator, but I actually hate thinking about money. I prefer to stay at arm's length, because I am easily rattled by the complexity of the numbers. But it helps to be aware of your own shortcomings: if I were to dig into our financial planning, it would lead me to paralysis and inaction. I need to stay closer to the creative side of things. The numbers on big events, once you get to know them, are unexpected. Would you guess that the flooring we had to put down to cover the turf at Tim Hortons Field football stadium cost north of six figures? That's a big number, and I have a hard time reconciling the ins and outs, so I try to keep my business calculations as simple as possible: Don't hire out for things that you can do yourself. Try to sell a few more tickets than you did the last time. Don't fly first class. Share a hotel room if you must. Be suspicious of comfortable things for as long as possible. And keep booking shows.

After we played a sold-out show at Scotiabank Arena in Toronto in 2019, our agent, Jack, recalled that of all the remarkable moments of the night, the one thing that amused him the most was that no one in the band ever pulled him aside to talk about how much money we were making. He said that it was totally expected for a band to want to talk about it on the night of their biggest show to date. But it never happened. And it's never really happened. We try to make any show we're playing—whether it's a club for two hundred people or an arena for fifteen thousand—the best show possible. And we trust the money will keep showing up. I don't know what we made that night in Toronto, but I assume it was more than $80.

SUPERSTITIONS

"Where and how do I work best?" is a simple question I hadn't really asked myself until recently. But it's a good one! The answer, after all, should bring me closer to the thing I'm always chasing: to create with a sense of joy and wonder in a way that keeps me entertained and moves the ball forward. I used to be superstitious about my work, imagining that an array of invisible forces would help complete the next song or give us our next big break, but I have come to realize this is delusional. I've learned that completing anything is just about old-fashioned hard work. Progress comes with some structure, and structure can look different to each person. When getting down to work, I'm attempting to declutter my mind and to sharpen my routine, so I have the best chance of having a good day.

There is a fine, but important, line between a routine and a superstition. Superstitions rely on *magic* to create outcomes. Routines, however, like good habits, take magic out of the equation. While an unseen connection to the universe is an undeniable part of creating anything, I feel that we attribute a misleading amount of mysticism to how art gets made. When Paul McCartney described how "Yesterday" was written, he famously explained that it came to him in a dream. This is unhelpful. I'm more interested in the *real* nuts and bolts of his process.

There's no one rule when it comes to setting yourself up to start a creative project. Everyone is different, and you should expect your process to evolve. For me, the ingredients for a productive day start early and with a clear mind. I crave a good night's sleep, followed by a coffee while reading a physical newspaper. I try to ease myself into the day, away from a screen or outside stimuli. I know emails and social media will consume other parts of the day, so it's not the first thing I need to look at.

Once I'm properly caffeinated, I'm excited to talk to people. I like to go on a morning "thinking walk" with Ash and chat about what we will try to accomplish that day. I'm looking forward to the next meeting, band practice, or phone call. I want to be close to people. For this book, I much preferred to write in a coffee shop, where the hustle and bustle stimulates the writing. I did very little writing at home in silence. Some of the best creative breakthroughs for this book came from walks and phone calls with friends. No matter the day, or where I am in the world, I am always on the hunt for something that might spark a new creative idea. I'll Shazam a song I hear while I'm out running errands or hum a melody into a voice note and put it away for later. Every interaction might lead somewhere interesting. These are all parts of my routine that engage my mind and energize my creative flow.

When I first started to play in bands, I spent a lot of time in music stores. I would go in and try out acoustic and electric guitars that I could not afford. I spent countless hours agonizing how to purchase an instrument that was imperative to my impending success as a musician. It was all cart-before-the-horse stuff: if I only had the $2,800 to afford that Gibson J-45, everything would come together. I somehow imagined the gear itself would make people take my songs more seriously. I also assumed it would make me practise my instrument more—which is untrue. You either have the desire to practise, or you don't. Of course, there are some musicians who love nothing more than diving into the big wide (and expensive) world of gear. The quality of their instrument is important and essential to their creative expression. They love the chase of finding the perfect vintage piece, the negotiation with the seller, and the victory of buying it. I can't handle any of it. It all feels like *work* to me.

I find the spark of connection I have with a passing instrument to be more fruitful. Picking up someone else's guitar or sitting at a new keyboard always does something different to my brain. It helps me in my job as a songwriter, as the unpredictable sounds open my mind to new ideas. And new ideas are what I'm after. Ironically, one of my favourite places to start a song is in a music store. There are so many random sounds happening, and nobody is really listening to anyone else. For me, a successful visit to a music store is coming up with a song and buying nothing.

I've learned to embrace wonky pianos and odd guitars. If they are easy to play and borderline functional, it doesn't matter if they are a little out of tune. The piano in my house *can't* stay in tune. Some of the keys are broken. The damper pedal doesn't work. I bought it off a friend for $400, and I wouldn't be able to resell it if I tried. But I love it. It's been the best musical purchase I've ever made. I love the ragtime-sounding overtones. I love the action of the keys them-selves—they're so easy and light to the touch. To my ears, the wonkiness covers my mistakes and makes my composi-tions a little more interesting.

As you can probably tell, when I'm preparing for any cre-ative endeavour—our concerts, a new song, or this book— I make every effort to avoid all superstitious instincts. For musicians, it's easy to approach your instrument and wonder if the universe is on your side and if the time is right. Supersti-tions can come in the form of many excuses that don't help much: "What microphone am I using? Is my special guitar around? Do I feel connected to my emotions right now? Do I need to go on a life-changing trip?" Stop it.

The act of shedding every possible material yearning was a turning point for me. If I had a melody, or phrase, or a couple of chords, I decided it didn't matter if I was near my *lucky* guitar or piano. *Any* guitar or piano would do. Once I made that shift, songwriting became less about frivolous contemplation and more about execution. I came to understand that an idea didn't need to be perfect; I just had to believe in a little nugget and hope it was something I could build upon. I could make that shitty little voice note and start playing with it in real life.

Putting yourself out there to make and create something great can be daunting. But the moment you start making excuses as to why you're not ready to create, I suggest you ask yourself if you're letting some superstition get in the way of the path ahead. Are you putting things off for another day because you've convinced yourself that the conditions aren't right? If your routine isn't serving you in the moment, then change it. If the place you typically write music isn't offering the right energy, find a new physical space to create. If the guitar you normally write with isn't sparking any joy, try a new one.

But—there is *one* moment of magic I've allowed myself to believe is part of our success. It's a tradition of sorts, but it does fall into the category of superstition. Like a basketball team about to hit the court, I do not want the band to go onstage without a hands-in cheer. Moments before our show starts, the band and crew assemble, as I start hooting and hollering for everyone to join the huddle. Once everyone is in, I hand the proceedings to Mike D.: "Mikey, what do we got tonight?" Without any thought, Mike says the first thing that comes to his mind. It's often vaguely related to the city we're in or a topical news item or some terrible pun. And that is the cheer. The cheer is so utterly forgettable I couldn't even tell you one single cheer in the history of our band, and we've done it at every single show we've ever played. And even though I know better, I enjoy this tradition because—no matter the size of the crowd—I need to believe it'll lead to the most transcendent and magical show of our lives.

KNOCK KNOCK

All creative ideas are some kind of reaction. A reaction to some small, mundane thing I've observed or a feeling I've had. Sometimes it's a reaction to the last thing I did because I don't want to repeat myself. Sometimes it's a reaction to the moment I'm in. Fraught political times have long been a source of inspiration for songwriters, and in January 2017, there was no shortage of material presenting itself. Donald Trump was about to be sworn in as the president of the United States, and shortly after the release of our fourth album, *Morning Report*, Arkells headed out for an American tour.

Our first stop on the tour was ground zero: Silver Spring, Maryland, a suburb of Washington, D.C. It would be the beginning of a full American run, where we'd open for U.K. punk rock balladeer Frank Turner, and it just so happened we landed in the nation's capital the day before Trump's inauguration. The heavy security presence spanned the city. In a place that is accustomed to motorcades, protests, and social justice activity, there was an eerie, sombre, and joyless feeling in the air.

Like our fans, Frank Turner's audience is politically engaged. There's a nod to social justice in the music, and the spirit of the shows is about love, kindness, and the acceptance of all stripes. Frank, a preacher-like punk icon, had the crowd sweaty and hoarse by the end of his set. Like the great rock stars before him, he demanded that we all do better if we wanted to see change in the world. For those two hours, the show offered comfort and the sense of community—*real-world comfort*—that we'd all been searching for in previous months.

The Women's March was the following day, and it was the first time since the election that I felt some sense of optimism. Seeing millions of people peacefully take the streets across the United States and around the world reminded me there were plenty of strangers out there with shared values. The images from the march were breathtaking. After that day, the shows we played became more like a rallying cry. The audiences on the tour, largely shook up from the election, used the shows as a spiritual release.

When we got home from that tour in February, I felt compelled to write about what the Women's March had offered during a dark time. Reacting to the moment. Being there had stirred up something in me, so I listened to the feeling. It was a feeling of relief, really. Relief in the idea that leadership could come not from one person but thousands banded together.

Tim sent me a bunch of drum loops and beats that he had recorded at home, and I scrolled through to see if anything grabbed my ear. There was one beat that felt particularly unique. It had this militaristic snare drum roll but with a rock 'n' roll swagger. The beat was aggressive and fast, yet soulful and smart. I started thinking about the shows we had been playing over the past month and wrote:

And in this collective, I got a brand-new perspective
Some news that might break the tension:
Can't walk on water but I'm walking through an intersection.
All aboard, I heard my sister sing
All aboard, and bring your offerings

I titled the demo "Knocking At The Door." Like most of our demos, I laid down the first verse, pre-chorus, and chorus and put it aside. We were actively promoting *Morning Report*, with a full year of touring ahead, and there were no plans to get back in the studio. But a week later, a professional opportunity presented itself, which demanded a reimagining of how we might want to work.

Any full-time working artist keeps their head on a swivel. One part of the day you're lost in creative thought, working on your next song, and the next moment, you're on the phone with your manager or agent making plans for the future. I enjoy both parts of the job, as they each require team building and all the interpersonal stuff that I find energizing. But I understand that it's the art that leads the way. To me, when we get news of a festival offer or good publicity, I only ever conceive of it as a conduit to keep happily working on the stuff I care about, which is the art. The songs. The show.

In the back end of the music business, artists and their management teams are constantly pitching songs for commercial use, but the hit rate is very low. In March, we had heard through the grapevine that Budweiser—a title sponsor of the Toronto Blue Jays—was looking for the right song to pair with their national ad campaign to kick off the Jays' season. Since our first album, Arkells had developed a natural kinship with the world of sports. Our tunes had been regularly used in broadcast montages, they had been licensed for video games, and they were often heard through speakers in baseball and football stadiums.

While I hoped we might land the commercial spot with one of the songs from *Morning Report*, the prospects didn't look promising. We'd heard from Budweiser that they didn't hear a musical fit, and deep down I agreed. Nothing on the album fit the mock-up of the ad we'd seen. So, we tried something new: as a Hail Mary, we sent along a ninety-second rough demo of "Knocking At The Door." We heard back from their team right away and arranged a lunch to discuss the project.

At the meeting, to our surprise, we were presented with the spot set to the unfinished version of "Knocking At The Door." We were told the campaign was moving ahead with the song, which we welcomed with excitement. We'd never landed a look as big as this before. But there was a problem: the song wasn't finished. To me, it was hardly a real song yet! We sat at the table, nodding and smiling and agreeing to the concept in principle. We understood that in a business where cutting through the culture is challenging at best, the opportunity was too good to pass up, but the timeline seemed almost impossible. The date was March 11, and the commercial needed to come out on April 7. A three-week turnaround was unprecedented.

While the opportunity was discussed, I quietly wondered if Budweiser had picked up on the song's subject matter and debated if a song about the Women's March could also be used as a sports anthem. I was curious to see how it would all go. The fan response to an artist licensing their music to a brand for a commercial has evolved over time. In the nineties, the notion of "selling out" was commonplace, and a rock band might've lost fans if their song was paired with a campaign. But by the aughts, things had evolved. The most successful and critically adored musicians were celebrated for landing an Apple commercial, as it was seen as a tool that could help break an entire career. We left the meeting and immediately started working the phones.

We called our label, Universal, and told them to pause plans to service our next single. In what I can only imagine was a confusing onslaught of communication, we told them we were changing course, had a new priority track (that they'd never heard or heard of), and we'd present a whole new marketing plan in a matter of days, while we also . . . wrote the rest of the song.

Our plan for bringing "Knocking At The Door" to life was (and still is) an insane timeline. It reminded me of what I like about the ethos of hip-hop: music is often conceived, created, and released quickly. It also foreshadowed the speed the music industry moves today, where unpredictable cultural moments can change timelines on a dime. At the time, though, the setup for most song releases—if you wanted to do it right—was months. But we understood that the opportunity was bigger than anything our label would be able to line up and execute.

In my experience, a studio can be a boring place, the trial and error in creation requires patience, and when you're one member in a five-piece band (not to mention the additional musicians involved), you wind up spending a lot of time waiting around. It's natural to feel like you are sometimes losing creative momentum—especially when you're working on an album that might take months to complete. But this was different: the energy was electric. The timeline added to the sense of urgency and excitement. We knew the track would see the light of day in a matter of weeks.

Musically speaking, "Knocking At The Door" is one of our most complex songs. It starts with the chorus groove from Tim's signature snare roll. The verse is half-time, which leads back into Tim's groove for the chorus. There's a solemn trumpet one moment, and a big brass section the next. With many moving parts, we worked through the arrangement together, figuring out each of the sections in real time.

The most perplexing part of the song was the bridge. Typically, when you write and record a song, the tempo remains the same throughout. In "Knocking At The Door," however, the song asked for something different. In an unprecedented move for our band, we changed the tempo *mid-song*. Sometimes, we've learned, you must listen to what the song *needs* and adjust accordingly.

> *From the ground up, from the people*
> *Turn the sound up, like we mean it*
> *Rise up! Rise up!*

As that section evolved, it built to a crescendo that naturally picked up speed, offering a new tempo for the final chorus. Although most listeners wouldn't notice, the final chorus is faster than the first two choruses. So much of the song bucks the conventions of pop music, but it's the result of the environment in which it was created and recorded. A reaction.

While all of this was happening, Ash was planning the music video and marketing, amid a schedule that was already stacked before we had decided to reinvent . . . everything we had planned.

I looked back to see if the timeline was as crazy as I remembered. This is what Ash mapped out for us:

March 9:	Meeting with Budweiser
March 13–15:	Record the song
March 24–26:	Film the music video
April 2:	Travel to Ottawa to attend and perform at the JUNO Awards broadcast
April 7:	Surprise release of "Knocking At The Door"

| *April 11:* | Commercial debuts during Blue Jays home opener. Play campaign launch event in Vancouver, B.C. |
| *April 15:* | Festival performance at Coachella in Indio, California |

When the song and music video dropped, it was a surprise to our fans, but a welcome one. For any fan who loved the more rock 'n' roll part of our sound, "Knocking At The Door" scratched that itch. But it also didn't feel like we were retreading past sounds and ideas. It all felt fresh, modern, and a step up from anything we had done before. A few days later, the commercial debuted to kick off the Blue Jays season, and we were off to the races.

The song had a remarkable journey for the next eighteen months. It was the number one song on alternative rock radio for fourteen weeks in Canada. We played it that summer at our first-ever headlining show at Budweiser Stage. It became an essential closer of our live set. That summer we performed it on television at the NHL Awards in Las Vegas and at the iHeartRadio MuchMusic Video Awards, where we won Fan Fave Video.

Every honest song starts in the same humble place, and every song is hoping to get the chance to be heard one day. Many great songs don't get their day in the sun. The success of "Knocking At The Door" started with music that was compelling but emerged because so many other lucky things aligned. We're grateful for the ride it took us on. Beyond the initial burst, the song has ended up in so many surprising places outside the world of sports. Because of its reach, the song's been adopted by striking union workers, students heading to write their final exams, and as the celebratory anthem of a patient completing their final round of chemotherapy.

With time, we've realized that no two songs will have the same journey. Every band, song, and performance live in their own moment in time, with their own context. But the lessons from "Knocking At The Door" are still useful. Write your best song and take that lunch meeting.

MAX, MEET MAX

In April 2017, we played Coachella. It was exciting for all the reasons that Coachella should be exciting: our name was on the poster, there was exceptional people-watching in every direction, and we got to enjoy some Southern California weather after a long Canadian winter.

As if playing the festival wasn't enough, we ran into Travis Barker at Whole Foods, caught glimpses of Mac Miller and Ariana Grande on a golf cart, and learned that The Weeknd and Selena Gomez had watched our set. Late in the evening, we even saw Leonardo DiCaprio, with a baseball hat pulled low, dance his ass off in the crowd.

Of all the stars we encountered at the festival, though, the meeting I went home to tell everyone about involved someone that nobody recognized and who might've spent the entire weekend completely unbothered, if he hadn't been noticed by me.

On Friday night, as the headliner was wrapping up their set, I saw a handsome Swedish man in his mid-forties standing by himself. It looked like Max Martin, the famed songwriter and producer. I could barely contain my excitement and wondered if I should bother the guy. I quickly determined that this was my moment.

Born and raised in Sweden, Max Martin is responsible for more number one hits than anyone in pop music history. For over twenty-five years, he has co-written and produced songs for Britney Spears, Backstreet Boys, Katy Perry, Taylor Swift, The Weeknd, and many more. He has helped launch the careers of our most iconic pop stars and offered a burst of new life to music legends who've needed fresh material. As a millennial, his music was the soundtrack of my childhood. So many of the songs he's worked on have become classics, touching listeners of all ages, in every corner of the world.

Beyond the wonder his songs inspired in the moment, his longevity is stunning. Historically, most renowned music producers have a window of a handful of years of hit-making before trends move on and another sound takes over. Somehow, he's remained at the top of the mountain for nearly three decades. Max Martin understands the demanding scope of the challenge and what it takes to remain excited about the work. This is the result, he would claim, of continuing to work with younger talent that keeps him sharp. He is the first to note that the success of any one song does not rest on his shoulders alone. A Max Martin production is often a group effort, with the artist and an illustrious handpicked team of expert writers and producers helping to shape the song.

As a fan, I'd spent hours wondering about the specifics of his process, but surprisingly there is little known about it. Despite his impact on popular music, Max Martin has only given a handful of interviews over the course of his career, appearing to have little interest in becoming a public figure. He'd prefer to let the music do the talking.

On that Friday night at the festival, I walked over and introduced myself. It was in fact him, and I quickly got to work and spent fifteen minutes peppering him with every question I could muster about how he does his work. I asked how certain parts of my favourite songs were written. He answered very specifically and patiently. When I brought up Katy Perry's recent single, "Chained to the Rhythm," a political anthem of sorts bundled in a dance groove, he explained that they wrote it the day after the 2016 presidential election. It wasn't a chart-topper, but I still loved the nuances of the production and appreciated knowing its origins even more. Even though "Chained to the Rhythm" wouldn't be considered his greatest accomplishment, I found it interesting that he and a pop star made the attempt to write something politically nuanced. Part of what makes Martin's music so exciting is that each song is a reaction to the music and culture of the moment.

Next, I inquired about the New Zealand pop star Lorde. That weekend Lorde was performing at Coachella, and there had been a big feature on her in the *New York Times* where she mentioned a recent conversation with Max Martin. She had released her new single "Green Light," and although she and Martin hadn't worked together, she still sought his opinion about the song before its release. As a matter-of-fact Swede, he offered a straightforward opinion. He said the song was an example of "incorrect songwriting." When I read this, I laughed: *incorrect songwriting* is a funny way to offer feedback to a global pop star. But I had understood what he meant. The song's form is unusual; on the first listen, there are transitions between parts that feel somewhat unconventional for a traditional pop song. For me it was validating to hear Martin confirm a musical instinct that I felt but didn't know how to articulate.

According to Lorde, Martin "had a very specific opinion, which had to do with melodic math." She clarified that it wasn't meant to be an insult; Martin just felt he was sharing the facts. A transcendent pop song, if that was the goal, shouldn't be hard for the listener to understand. I asked Martin about it. He became somewhat animated in his response: "I thought we were having a private conversation! I didn't think she'd quote me in the *New York Times*!" The goal of songwriting for him—and the reason he gets approached by the biggest stars in the world—is to deliver surefire hit songs. Songs that are played in bars for decades to come. My impression was that he wasn't sure "Green Light" possessed the tightly executed touchstones of her breakout single, "Royals."

Of course, despite what Max Martin says about what's *correct*, the inspiring thing about music and art is that there is no such thing as a right answer. It's all subjective, and we all have different tastes. And our tastes can change. But as a student of songwriting, I've spent every day since I was a teenager thinking about transcendent songs and how writers pull off their ideas. How they can pack so much brilliance into three minutes of music. How the alchemy of words, melody, and rhythm can work together *just right*.

In our modest little world of Arkells indie rock, the stakes aren't the same as they are for Max Martin, but the pressure is similar. It's not the external pressure I'm talking about, but the pressure that comes from within. I've always felt a lot of responsibility to bring the band good material. It's my main job, and I don't want to let the band down. With every album, I want to make sure I'm delivering something that everyone is pumped and proud to work on.

After Anthony joined the band and we worked with producers Tony Hoffer and Eric Ratz on *High Noon*, my conception of how we could write songs slowly changed. I began to sense there was an endless array of equally valid approaches to the task. If I remained open to new ideas and collaborators, I sensed my education could be limitless too. But first, I had my own mental hurdle to get over.

For the first three records, our band had never worked with outside songwriters, because I was stuck on the idea that it was an unethical practice for a *real* band. This was a silly rule I made up based on a small sample of bands that I liked, who would never work with outside songwriters. Co-writing, after all, seemed to be a thing reserved for pop acts, not scrappy artists.

I was wrong. In 2015, after an extended bout of suspicion and apprehension about working with professional songwriters, I arrived in Los Angeles, the epicentre of the music business, for my first co-writing trip. There are plenty of music hubs around the world, but the most concentrated and diverse talent pool is in L.A. If you want to get into banking, you go to New York City. If you have a mind for tech, you go to San Francisco. If you have ambition and musical chops, there's a good chance you'll try working in L.A. Not only do many musicians relocate there, but others like me will go for a week to write and learn.

On my first day, I picked up lessons that still inform my practice. I arrived at a little studio that belonged to John Fields. The only thing I knew about John was that he had an impressive resumé, which included collaborations with rock 'n' roll bands like Jimmy Eat World and pop stars like the Jonas Brothers. We got to work immediately. I showed him a rough idea that I had started the day before, which was still missing a chorus. Without too much discussion, we started laying things down. He suggested we start the chorus on an F-major chord and sing a high note I never would've considered because I thought it was out of my range. I was unsure of the idea, but John began to coach me through it. He explained that if I really leaned in, I'd be able to get there, and the chorus would soar. I quickly jotted out some lyrics that felt a little trite—placeholders—but John thought they were great and insisted we keep them. The real-time analysis of my work from an impartial expert was invaluable. "Yes, keep that." "No, doesn't quite feel right." "Let's try something else."

When it came time to record the vocal, he told me to sing the song right there next to him, with the speakers playing the instrumental back at us. I paused, thinking I'd misheard him and pointed to the vocal booth, because . . . that's where singers go? Nope! John insisted I sing it right there next to him at his computer. He explained that Bono is often known to sing right in the control room with everyone hanging out. Being around other people makes his performance more natural, and the slight bleed from the instrumental track would be irrelevant in the end. All that really mattered, in John's opinion, was getting a good performance. After ten years of recording Arkells songs from an isolated vocal booth and being so focused on the sound from a technical perspective, I learned the opposite approach could also work—and even improve the final product.

Within about an hour we had written the beginnings of "My Heart's Always Yours," and I left with an amazing demo in my pocket. "My Heart's Always Yours" is considered one of our most heartfelt romantic songs. It's been played at many weddings as the soundtrack to the first dance and has an authentic emotional resonance because it comes from a real place—and in large part, I think, because of the new approach that I learned from John. That day taught me a lot about how to capture a spark and run with it. How to be instinctive. How to stop thinking and try to find what feels right. There was something about being on the clock that seemed counterintuitive to creation, but I think has merit. It gets your brain working in a different way when there is less time for contemplation. Once an idea is down on paper, you have more time to examine it with distance and perspective. Sometimes the idea is better than you think.

In 2019, hoping to learn more, I went on another set of writing blind dates with some producer-writers in L.A. I went straight from the plane to the neighbourhood of Van Nuys and pulled up to a shoddy-looking one-storey to find two guys around my age chatting. As I approached, I overheard a discussion related to a news item from the NBA subreddit that day. I introduced myself to two guys who turned out to be the producers I'd be writing with, Tom Peyton and Ryan Spraker. I quickly learned their workflow was the opposite of John Fields's, but just as compelling. They were very funny and comforting to be around as well as musically talented, suggesting ideas I never would've thought of.

During these sessions with Tom and Ryan, I was flummoxed: I'd arrive at eleven a.m. and nothing would happen for hours. They would chat and surf the internet. There was laughter. There were jokes. There were deep philosophical conversations about love and life, and intense discussions about basketball. Nothing moved at the pace I was used to. After a couple hours, Tom would suggest we get lunch. On the first day, after a few hours of hanging around, I interjected, "Guys, can we do some fucking work?" Tom looked at me with a grin. "Slow down, Max! We will get there. You gotta chillllll."

Finally, around three p.m. stuff would slowly begin to happen. Ryan would be fiddling with the guitar or piano, and somebody would say something to spark an idea. Tom would start singing something with made-up words over whatever Ryan was looping on the piano. I'd start singing random things. The words often had something to do with what had come up earlier in the conversation. We weren't searching for the right puzzle pieces; the puzzle itself was being created in the moment.

Tom, I learned, was practising *disengagement* by appearing to not do any work for the first three hours. It seemed counterintuitive, but when you're actively *not* working, I learned, your mind starts to do unpredictable things. Your fingers on the keyboard might produce something unexpected. And when you're not thinking about how to cram a certain set of lyrics in over the music, you might come up with an interesting melody that takes things in a new direction. Spontaneous words might begin to take shape, and a new narrative might unfold. This is how we started songs like "You Can Get It" and "Past Life." They both began with just a piano loop and lots of rambling melodies. We also began songs like "Nowhere To Go" and "All Roads" based on soulful instrumentals that Anthony and Mike had sent me. These experiences reminded me that a new song can start anywhere if you're keeping your ears open to something that feels grabby.

Above all, the goal of these co-writing sessions is learning how to write honest music that feels good to the ear. And that's what I've learned from professionals. There are technical components you can discuss—are certain melodies and rhythms too repetitive or not repetitive enough?—but they all get at what Max Martin is after. And what The Beatles did so well. And what Motown understood. In a rare interview, Max Martin said that when he shows a friend a new song he's working on, he pays attention to their body language. Are they engaged with the music, or are they looking at their phone by the second verse? It's a binary question. Does it move you, or does it not?

Of course, I've experienced other songwriting sessions where the ideas were hard to find, and nothing clicked. But failure offers lessons for the next time too. When I head to a session, the exercise is about finding something musical I might not have discovered otherwise, and to have something exciting to bring back to the band. New experiences inevitably bring something interesting to light and help for the next time. These days, songs can start anywhere. Sometimes it's just me at the piano, or an instrumental piece from a bandmate, or in a room with a few songwriting strangers. And I can enjoy them all for different reasons.

In 2022, I had a reunion with Max Martin in Toronto. A musical called & Juliet, a reimagining of Romeo and Juliet, came to Toronto's Princess of Wales Theatre. It's a modern tale where Juliet decides to not kill herself and instead reclaims her life, empowered by the virtues of feminism. It's a rollicking adventure set entirely to the music of Max Martin. Hits from the Backstreet Boys, Britney Spears, Ariana Grande, and many more provide the soundtrack. I went with my family, and we were all dancing by the end. It's one of the best musicals I've ever seen.

Just before the show began, Max Martin walked down the aisle. It was two days before the official opening night, and as the producer of the show he was there to watch and offer notes. By this point in my life, you'd think I'd have experienced enough encounters with Arkells fans to know how to conduct myself in this situation. I *wouldn't* do the thing that well-meaning fans often do: "Hey, Max! Remember? Calgary?

We talked outside of the coffee shop in 2012? It's me, Trevor!"
Well, that is exactly what I did to Max Martin. I hopped up
from my seat, tapped him on the shoulder, and said, "Max!
It's me, Max! We talked at Coachella? Backstage, after the
headliner? Remember?"

He stared blankly back at me, lacking context. A matter-
of-fact Swede, he could not lie to me.

TICKET COUNTS

After all these years, tracking ticket counts is the one aspect of being a touring musician I can't quite stomach. Despite my curiosity and involvement with just about every other part of the business, I simply can't look at the numbers.

In the early days of working with a booking agent, I learned they'd routinely send along a spreadsheet reporting on the present ticket sales of the tour. The final column—the one that would haunt me—read "percentage sold" to date. If the band was set to be playing a venue with a capacity of one thousand and we'd sold three hundred tickets, then the number would read 30 percent. Simple math, right? But the issue with this, for me, is that the percentage sold number was mostly humiliating. You're no longer grateful for the people in some far-off place who cared to buy a ticket. You're thinking about the number in the percentage sold column and how you wished it was higher. There is little dignity in the exercise. And if you ask any musician what they want, it's some dignity in their job and to work with some sense of pride and optimism.

I learned how degrading tracking ticket counts could be during an early period of our career when we were between managers, and I was working directly with our agent, Jack, on one of our Canadian tours. The venues we booked were bigger than the clubs we'd played on the previous tour. We were hopeful the band could keep growing our audience. The ambitious tour immediately sold more tickets than our previous on-sale (the term for sales numbers on the first day), so you'd think I would have been happy. I was not happy. I was in agony. For the following weeks and months as the tour approached, the percentage in the final column moved along at a snail's pace. It started around 30 percent and might take a few weeks to get to 40 percent and so on. There were some shows in bigger markets like Vancouver that sold out quickly, but in smaller places like Regina and Winnipeg, I'd scan the column and feel like we had made a terrible miscalculation. Why did we ever believe that we should be playing in a larger venue? I'd read the number as if it was a grade in school: 40 percent was a failing mark.

As the tour approached, I began to dread those shows. I felt responsible for dragging the band out on the road. Even worse, I felt embarrassed for all the people who bought tickets to one of those shows. Who wants to see a band in what is basically an empty room?

But then this thing happened every time we walked on stage: it didn't look so bad! I'd look out on a sea of faces who were excited to be there. It turns out if you sell five hundred tickets in a club that can hold one thousand people, it looks and feels pretty good. There were moments in the night when I'd peer into the dark empty corners at the back of the room and begin to feel sorry for myself, but for the most part, it all went much better than I could've imagined. Booking the right rooms is a constant dance. We could've had the satisfaction of having a sold-out tour in four-hundred-capacity rooms, but it's the bigger swing that requires more belief and strategy.

What makes me feel a little better in moments of embarrassment and dread is remembering that every artist in the world suffers from some version of the same feeling. I've heard Chris Martin from Coldplay admit that ticket counts can still ruin his day. He joked that regardless of all the global suffering in the news, a bad ticket report for a show in, say, Pittsburgh would become all-consuming, despite—and fully aware of—how ridiculous that sounds. Coldplay has been one of the highest-grossing live acts for the last two decades, but the feeling doesn't leave him. I've heard that Springsteen plays smaller shows in Brazil, because he hasn't toured there as much, and I wonder how he compares himself to some other American acts that do *real* business down there. Sometimes I imagine the only person who must feel on the top of the mountain is Paul McCartney. He's unanimously considered the most important songwriter of our lifetime. But then again, even if he's able to avoid the anxiety of ticket sales, I'm sure he lives with the insecurity that half of The Beatles fans think he's no John Lennon.

After spending that tour tormented over ticket sales, I told the band and our team that I do not want to know ticket counts ever again. Some artists can handle it. I cannot. Now, everyone knows to keep me off those emails and not to mention the numbers when I'm in the room. For me, it is a matter of self-preservation. Everyone needs their own boundaries, and those are mine. The only time I want to know about a show's ticket sales is if it's sold out so we can make a social media post about it and carry on. Otherwise, I'll assume that every show needs a bit more work.

IT'S IN THE DETAILS

Performing in a touring band is an odd existence for many reasons, but it's the arc of the day that is the most unusual. There are two concentrated hours—the show—when the intensity of the work is unlike anything else. The rest of the day, if you're not paying attention, can be some combination of long, boring, and directionless. Every morning, I wake up in the next city, grab my morning coffee, and reflect on the previous night's show. I think about what worked and what didn't and how we might improve the next one.

In 2016, our tour arrived in Halifax, Nova Scotia, for a show at the Forum. By this point, we'd played Halifax a handful of times, and I was ruminating on how we could make this concert the best one yet. I decided to call my friend Mike Veerman as I walked around the downtown that morning.

Traditionally, I work best when talking things out, and that day I was thinking about how I'd convey our fondness for the city of Halifax onstage. I wanted to offer a personal anecdote about our relationship to the town, but the monologue I was writing in my head kept running into dead ends. The shape of the storytelling wasn't quite right—it was too wordy and probably needed a punchline. I knew I couldn't quite solve the task on my own, so I thought I'd try and work it out with Mike.

With any creative puzzle, it's best to approach the person who'd most enjoy the challenge. Talking about *anything*—sports, movies, relationships—with Mike is a unique joy. He's not only a sympathetic listener and willing helper; he's also the best storyteller I know. Sit with him in a pub for a few hours, and he'll become the centrepiece of any group conversation, asking questions and regaling the entire table with stories. In his twenties, he was the charismatic singer of a band, and he has had a career writing and producing ads and television. And he loves comedy. *Saturday Night Live. Late Night.* As a fan, he can keenly dissect why something works onstage or on the page or why it doesn't.

On the phone, I described my problem: I am long-winded. I ramble. Broadly, I know what I want to convey with my stage banter, but when I start to talk without practising, I meander and stumble, and my stories begin to feel directionless. I might be the one onstage in charge of doing the singing and the talking, but that's not necessarily because I'm the best at it. It's because I grabbed the microphone first. When I speak to the crowd, my goal is to finish every story with a bang.

I started by spitting out some basic ideas for Mike. In no particular order, I was rhyming off themes. I wanted to tell everyone who came to the show that they were welcome and should feel at home. I wanted to mention a local bar that Arkells have played at in the past—the Seahorse Tavern—to remind the crowd of our history there. I wanted that night, our biggest concert in Nova Scotia to date, to feel like an intimate club show. Mike understood the tone and pacing that I was after. He started riffing, and I started typing stuff down on my iPhone:

> *There's all sorts of clubs out there . . . (pause)*
> *There's "exclusive" clubs . . . I never got invited to those!*
> *Fancy clubs with bottle service . . . that I can't afford . . .*
> *There's rock 'n' roll clubs—like the Seahorse down the road.*
> *But there's one club I know we can all get into—it's the*
>   *Halifax Forum for Arkells!*

Mike would be the first to say this isn't the most profound piece of banter, but it's thoughtful—and there are personalized details that might connect with the audience and make that show feel a little more special. If you look closely at the writing, there's more going on than you might think at first glance. There's repetition. I say *club* four times, before landing on the final *club*—our club. We have a play on words too. *Club* has two meanings here—it's a music venue but also a community. There's brevity. There are no unneeded words. The writing is tight. And there is a payoff at the end: we land on a triumphant moment that welcomes everyone to the show. There's a kind of math to the type of writing that Mike is incredibly attuned to. In Mike, I have my own script-writer—as if I'm hosting a TV show.

I began to rehearse and make my own edits. By showtime, I had something that felt original for the Halifax crowd. This ritual—walking around the day of the show and thinking about what I might say to the crowd that night (and calling Mike when I get stuck)—has become one of my favourite parts of being on tour. It gives some shape and purpose to the day. To some, this routine might sound like the opposite of sex, drugs, and rock 'n' roll, but to live like a 1970s rock star on tour would make me feel like I'm underserving the show that night. Mere mortals like myself would have short careers if we stuck to that script. I've always understood that I need to be attentive if I'm going to have any shot at being good. For every Fleetwood Mac tale of wild backstage she-nanigans, there are hundreds of pedestrian stories that rarely get told but are far more instructive.

The performers I've learned the most from find ways to actively add to their creative projects throughout their day, moving the ball forward with some intention.

A few years ago I had the opportunity to hang out with Shania Twain after a show in Toronto. The concert was a joy, and everyone who attended left feeling like they got their money's worth. She cared about the fans, pulling audience members onstage for spontaneous conversations and stories. Shania's voice remained spectacular in her mid-fifties. For the encore, she somehow donned the *original* leopard print outfit from the iconic "That Don't Impress Me Much" music video, which she sported over twenty-five years ago.

After the show, we headed backstage and spent an hour with Shania and her husband, Fred. I was curious to observe someone in such an intimate setting. She has accomplished every professional achievement in popular music and has lived much of her life in the public spotlight. I couldn't help myself: I took the opportunity to ask every question I could come up with. In a small room, as we drank wine, the inquisition began:

"What do you eat after a show?"

"How much do you sleep?"

"What do you listen to before you make an album?"

"What do you do when you're off the road?"

"What other tours and artists inspired this tour?"

Despite me turning this causal hang into what must've felt like an episode of *60 Minutes*, Shania was unfazed and answered all of my questions with enthusiasm. Of the many things I learned about her process, one task on her to-do list was to produce an original outfit for every single night of the tour. There were over *eighty* dates on the tour. She explained that she wanted every single person who attended a show to understand that their night would be special. A singular experience. She wanted to ensure that photos and videos from each show were different from the rest.

To do this, she designed each outfit. With her seamstress, they worked three to five shows in advance, making every single afternoon on tour the playground for a new art project. They would design it, order the materials, and construct it together. Shania could've outsourced this work but—like in so many parts of her career—felt it was important that she drive the creative. This little story stuck out to me because it's what makes the great ones *great*. Inventing projects that offer daily meaning. The desire to deliver at the highest level means paying attention to the little details of each show. Continuing to workshop when offstage. Even after selling out her world tour in advance, her focus remained on finding opportunities to squeeze every last drop out of the show.

In 2013, we toured across Canada with The Tragically Hip. One night, backstage around dinner time, I sat with Gord Downie, and he began casually telling a story about driving around Prince Edward County with his young son. He was explaining to his boy the virtues of rock 'n' roll, specifically why The Who were such titans. He began to describe how, in the apex of one of their signature songs, just as Roger Daltrey was about to let out a primal scream, it was *essential* to turn the volume up to eleven. The only way to grasp the power of what The Who were doing was to set the volume at *stun*. I was on the edge of my seat as Gord became growingly animated as he told the story, and I felt lucky he shared this little moment of his father-son bonding with me.

Later that night as I watched The Hip from side-stage, I heard something familiar. Mid-song, as Gord performed his signature spoken word diatribe, he began to tell the story about his father-son drive and The Who again! In classic "Gord," he had the audience entranced while the band jammed behind him, before letting out his *own* signature primal scream. I can't be certain if our dinner sparked the idea, or he was simply workshopping a bit on me, but I understood that casual conversations could become not only part of the show but his daily practice.

Feeling engaged in my role requires action, and I know it will never be readily served up to me. I have to go looking for solutions and new ideas. When we're on tour, we have one night in each city to make a lasting impression, and then we won't be back for a year or two. I don't want to leave anything on the table. I know it won't be perfect, but that's okay. That's not the point. The point is gradual improvement and that I'm offering my best work to the team and to the crowd every chance we get.

RALLY TIME

"So . . . are we going to talk about the elephant in the room? Or just continue to ignore it?" Mike D. inquired over lunch in Toronto. We had just finished a CityTV interview at an ice cream parlour and we were eating sandwiches from Black Camel at Ramsden Park off Yonge Street. Ash and I didn't really have a good answer, so we laughed nervously and muttered optimistic-sounding things. It had been ten years since the band put out our first record, and we were embarking on an idea more ambitious than anything we'd attempted before. After a year of planning, it seemed like it was all about to go sideways.

It was Wednesday, June 20, 2018, and there were just three days until we would play our biggest show ever, The Rally, a hometown festival we'd built brick by brick. We had chosen that weekend because excitement for summer in Southern Ontario would be peaking, and the weather is usually perfect. Over twenty thousand people were supposed to attend the show on Saturday night in Hamilton at the city's outdoor football stadium.

In reality there wasn't just one elephant in the room. There were two. The first elephant was the forecast: 100 percent chance of thunderstorms on Saturday night. Forecasts, as we know, aren't always correct, and Ash—looking to offer something positive—reminded us that we had access to the finest weather tracking technology to monitor the day. We might not be able to control the weather, but at least we'd feel productive by watching it obsessively. The other elephant in the room was a baby. A baby that hadn't been born yet. Anthony and his wife, Scarlet, had been expecting their first child the week prior, but there still wasn't any sign of the baby.

The weather part was somewhat less complicated. Rain? I could deal with rain. As long as there wasn't any lightning, we'd soldier on. We even had a song for the occasion, "A Little Rain (A Song For Pete)." I could envision it: the second song in, with a big ol' grin, I'd address the matter at hand directly to the crowd: "We sing this song on days of sunshine, and we sing this song on days of rain!" Then when the chorus kicked up, we'd all sing together: "When the rain starts coming down . . . a little rain ain't bringing me down!"

The baby part was genuinely confounding for me. I tried to stay optimistic. It would have to be an amazing coincidence for the baby to be born in the three-and-a-half-hour window of our show on Saturday. Quietly, I tried to reason with myself: What were the chances that, in this big old life, the baby would be born two weeks late at that very moment? With Scarlet ready for labour in Toronto, if that baby existed before seven thirty p.m. (to account for travel to Hamilton) or after eleven p.m., then we'd be just fine. I'm sure these are not the same calculations that would be made by impending first-time parents, but this was the math I was doing in *my* head. Anthony really could not be replaced—not even for a night.

On what was shaping up to be the biggest night of our career, things were not exactly sailing smoothly. So we tried to focus on the things we *could* control. And the reasons we decided to do the thing in the first place.

The location of the show meant a lot to us. The city of Hamilton is a core part of our band's story. The affection and pride we feel for the city, and the love we've received in return, has propelled us forward at every turn. The belief in and support for our band is akin to the affection you'd receive from a loving family. What makes it unique, however, is that *we chose* to make it our home. We all grew up in different parts of Southern Ontario, but McMaster University in Hamilton is where the band was born. During early shows, I couldn't declare from the stage, "We're Arkells from Newmarket, Mississauga, Guelph, London, and Toronto." That'd be confusing and clunky. So, when we applied to music festivals or created our Myspace page and were prompted to list our hometown, Hamilton was the simple truth: it's where we met, lived, and learned our craft. In many ways, The Rally was a thank-you and a celebration for the city that had nurtured us.

Not many large-scale shows had happened in Hamilton in the previous forty years. If you wanted to see one, you had to go to Toronto. The most memorable concert of local lore happened in 1975 when Pink Floyd performed at the old Ivor Wynne Stadium, then home of the Canadian Football League's Hamilton Tiger-Cats. Built in the middle of an east-end neighbourhood, Ivor Wynne was a perfect snapshot of Hamilton's yesteryear: smokestacks from the city's bustling steel factories visible a few blocks away, with locals converting their driveways into paid parking spots on game days. The Pink Floyd show, by all accounts, was a rowdy affair. During the show, the band's pyrotechnics blew out the scoreboard, people became obscenely drunk and disorderly, and the neighbours around the stadium were generally annoyed by the vulgarity of the whole thing.

Tim Hortons Field, where we were scheduled to play, was built right next to Ivor Wynne Stadium and opened in 2014. We hoped the day would be more than just a show, but a chance to shine a light on all the parts of the city that deserved a celebration. For five decades, downtown Hamilton had suffered the same economic fate as many Rust Belt industrial cities. But we revered the people—many who were friends of ours—who had the courage to open new businesses, who worked for civic social programs, and who fought for community-minded projects like affordable bike share programs and better health care for underserved communities.

We believed we could scale the stadium, selling tickets on the floor and the first level. If we could get to fifteen thousand tickets, the show would look and feel good and would be something to be proud of. With no concert infrastructure existing inside the football stadium, our promoter Erik Hoffman—who's hosted and organized every kind of large-scale concert and festival experience—explained it would be very expensive. We would have to bring in everything: staging, lighting, flooring to protect the turf, washrooms, barricades, to name only a few items on a very long list. To me, it all sounded like a grand experiment, a challenge we could sink our teeth into. The only question I had about the expenses: "Well, are we going to *lose* money?" He didn't think so. That was good enough for me.

Since we were inventing the damn thing, we could make The Rally whatever we wanted. We'd choose the line-up, invent the programming, and handle all of the marketing around the day. With every new choice, we asked ourselves, "Does it feel *like us*?" Whether it's a song, performance, or concert poster, does it feel like it's authentic to who we are? Asking these questions, and paying attention to the answers, is the best path to making something we feel we can stand behind.

If we were going to do it right, I knew we had to *really* lean into every detail. We connected with the Hamilton city council and asked if the city could extend its Ticket to Ride program, which would allow concertgoers to ride the city buses to and from the show safely and for free. With Hamilton Flea, we coordinated a local artist and food market, an inclusive environment around the stadium, free for anyone who wanted to check it out. In collaboration with PLUS1, a nonprofit that connects touring musicians with local charities, we ended up donating over $40,000 through ticket sales and private contributions to Refuge: Hamilton Centre for Newcomer Health, a clinic that largely serves the city's new immigrant community. A pet project for me was our partnership with Hamilton Bike Share: we planned a meet-up with an army of cyclists outside Jackson Square mall to ride four kilometres on the city's newly minted bike lanes that run along Cannon Street to Tim Hortons Field.

The whole experience illuminated a feeling that I've long had. The satisfaction I experience with an Arkells show is always beyond the music itself. It's the moments of connection that happen throughout the entire day. With The Rally, we could curate the experience for anyone who chose to be a part of it.

By Friday, the day before the show, the impending thunderstorm appeared. It can't be overstated how much bigger—and frankly jaw-dropping—the scope of the show was compared to anything else we had done up to that point as a band. The stadium seemed impossibly huge, and the rain made our final preparations that much more overwhelming. We had planned to soundcheck that evening, and the downpour complicated every logistic. We diligently put on our work boots and did our best to calmly run through the entire show, dodging puddles in the process and dealing with gusts of wind blowing the stage around. There weren't a lot of smiles, laughs, or horsing around. It was all business.

Amid the rainstorm, we did, however, get some good news. Scarlet had given birth to Oscar that morning, and she and the baby were happy and healthy. Anthony made it to our rainy soundcheck before heading right back to the hospital.

Once we received news of the birth, I felt like we were in the clear. It didn't matter what happened with the weather. If the band was together, we'd be okay.

On Saturday afternoon, the grey skies were spitting, but they didn't look menacing. The high-end weather trackers informed us it wouldn't get any worse, and by showtime the temperature would be 22 degrees Celsius and we'd have clear skies. A perfect night for a show. We took the stage at nine p.m., and I thought back to the advice our agent, Jack, had offered years ago when we'd played our first big theatre show at the Danforth Music Hall: "Remember the people in the back." If I had one job on that massive stage, it was to work every corner of the room.

I have two vivid memories of the show. The first was just pointing and waving a lot, a cartoon super-sized version of myself attempting to entertain that many people. The other happened during the bridge of our sentimental song "And Then Some," when I had the privilege of breaking the news to over twenty thousand people that Anthony Carone had just become a new dad. In the middle of the most intense and emotional week of his life, Anthony started crying happy tears. And then we all started crying. We normally don't have a moment to reflect in the middle of the show, but the feelings of gratitude and love for Scarlet and Oscar came pouring out.

Molly Hayes, Mike D.'s wife, has a wicked sense of humour and likes to call The Rally "Hamilton: The Musical." She says this with a smirk and a dash of pride, but she's not wrong. Arkells have always been an ensemble act, and this was our biggest ensemble performance yet. The Rally reminded us of an important lesson, one that will always stay with me: it's foolish to assume that things should go smoothly in the first place. When you're inventing an undertaking as ambitious as The Rally, the hurdles are an inevitable part of the experience. And that's okay. Because when you get to the other side of it, you're that much better for the next time.

MESSAGE BOARDS

You don't need to be a public person to be intimidated by the internet. Participating in any online conversation means potentially putting yourself in the line of fire of strangers and acquaintances. Many people, including myself, look to the internet for a sense of community and validation. For any working musician, online discourse has become part of the job, and it's prudent to be a savvy participant. But as an artist, especially in the beginning, the relationship between yourself and the internet can become intense, quickly.

My first encounter with an online forum happened in the mid-2000s, on a message board called Stillepost—a community for bands and fans of the Canadian indie rock scene. It was an early iteration of the internet, and when I discovered the site at the age of seventeen, I became obsessed with it. It was a resource for upcoming shows, announcements, and, most importantly, punditry. The natter came from users who were a little older and, in my mind, *much* cooler than me. I didn't know many of them in real life, but anyone who had a presence in the community seemed to embody the persona of, say, a vintage clothing store owner. You know the type: incredibly self-assured, great taste, and zero interest in pleasing anyone. I didn't post much, but I loved the mini dramas that played out between the most frequent contributors. The threads were usually about what bands were great, and who was shit, and who was deserving of more recognition. It was pre-Twitter but had the same rhythms and in-group/out-group behaviours we see online today.

I spent a lot of time worried about what those people thought of our band as we were getting started. My insecurities were all wrapped up in who I was as a person. I felt certain that I was a little too smiley and approval-seeking. I desperately wanted to be hipper and more detached, but I couldn't help but be who I was, which was sort of the opposite. The moment their imagined judgment came to mind, I'd become somewhat paralyzed and insecure. Every time I had a creative thought, I would immediately wonder how it might be perceived on Stillepost. It could be about *anything*. The shirt I was wearing onstage at the show? The title of a new song? My banter as I spoke to the audience? Any response I imagined would always come in the form of a snicker. Even to this day, if I run into people who were in that scene during that time, I still think about what they might say about our band on that message board (if it still existed). Many of them are teachers, real estate agents, or bartenders now and seem happy for the success of our band, but I can't help but wonder who might be rolling their eyes.

While my relationship with the internet is more measured today, it's not always easy to find a balance between enjoying it and fearing it. While I write this book, thinking about the potential commentary from online critics occasionally plagues me. It can briefly stall my writing. It's the freelance journalists on social media and the anonymous users in the comment section. I imagine their one-liners and quips for their audience to like and share. I can already see it: I predict how some relatively innocuous passage in this book could be taken out of context, and the devilish zinger that will put me in my place. It's inevitable. I've been aimed at before, and it's a jarring experience.

Beyond your own inner monologues that can derail any sense of self-worth, worrying about what other people think has just as much—maybe even more—power to inspire doubt. So I try to remember what's important to me: the creative work itself. It's one thing to be a critic; it's another to be the person who does the thing. And doing the thing has always felt to me like a better use of time than judging something else. It's the ultimate antidote to the vast assortment of criticisms, real or imagined. I try to remember a good piece of advice I heard long ago: some bands play for the people watching side-stage, and some play to the fans in the crowd who bought the ticket. I want to perform for the people who buy the ticket and want to be entertained.

When our band was coming up, we made an ongoing effort to win over industry gatekeepers. I was reminded of this chapter when I recently ran into an old friend named Leila. At first, I couldn't place her face, but she smiled, pointed at me, and in her British accent said, "Max! I know you! It's nice to see you again. I remember you well!"

She saw the look of confusion in my eyes. "It's Leila Hebden! You sat across from me at Sneaky Dee's in 2006. You slid a toonie across the table and said, 'This is 20 percent of what we made tonight at the show. If you want to be our manager, you can have your commission right now.'"

I blushed and immediately remembered who Leila was. When our band was in university and starting to gig around, I had heard of a mythical young British manager living in Toronto and working with the coolest Canadian bands. She helped them get signed to the hippest international indie labels and develop their careers. We didn't have a manager at the time, and I thought she could be the perfect fit. The bands that she managed were beloved on Stillepost, and I spent a lot of time thinking about how Arkells could win over someone like Leila.

Turns out Leila had moved back to London, started a family, and was eventually hired by the artist management division of Maverick, which manages Paul McCartney, Shania Twain, and Andrea Bocelli. After all these years, it was amazing to see how her career had evolved. She still had her tongue pieced, tattoos, and looked and acted every bit the *Leila* I remembered.

"You used to email me your songs *all the time*. I probably still have the emails."

I laughed and confirmed that, yes, that sounded like something that I would've done. Stillepost be damned—my determination always seemed to get in the way of *looking* cool.

"I've been following you and your rise. I'm so happy to see your success!" she said, as we shared a hug.

I could've sworn Leila didn't know me from a hole in the wall in 2006. That I was just one of many young musicians vying for her attention as she hung out and managed *the cool bands*. But Leila was probably never that. She was just a person like me, working away, trying to make sense of her own career. The Leilas I meet—who came up through a scene and have built lasting careers—have all worked diligently, built strong relationships, and treated others with respect. Those are the ones that seem to stick around.

When I look back on our career so far, I can laugh at all the precocious things that I've done, understanding that they came from a genuine desire to feel accepted. What makes me shudder is when I consider any time wasted getting derailed by the comment sections online. As disruptive as the internet can be, all of the nonsense evaporates quickly when you put down your phone and stop staring at the screen. With time, I've realized that everyone is just trying to build a decent life for themselves, and belabouring the fickle rhythms of the internet is largely unhelpful to your life in the real world.

SOMETHING IN THE AIR

If you're a self-employed person, the future can feel precarious, even at the best of times. It takes some blind faith and belief in yourself that you'll be rewarded for your hard work. At the worst of times, it requires deep persistence and creativity to keep the train on the tracks. Since working full-time as musicians, we've learned that live shows are the lifeblood of our business.

There was *one* particular gig in the calendar that I was excited for, because I'd have the chance to rub shoulders with some NBA legends. It was March 11, 2020, and it would be a night to remember, but not for the reasons I thought at the time. It would be seventeen months until we played another show.

At Hotel X in downtown Toronto, the Nick Nurse Foundation hosted a gala dinner where many players were in attendance to support Nick's efforts in helping underserved youth in sports, music, and literacy. Since becoming pals with Nick and joining the board of his foundation, Arkells were asked to perform as the headliner of the event. The added surprise of the night was that Nick himself would join us onstage at the piano for a few numbers.

The evening kicked off with the players arriving on a red carpet where press photographers awaited. We shook hands and smiled for the cameras with seven-footers Marc Gasol and Serge Ibaka, and we met some of Nick's family who'd come up for the event. Once the program began, I was asked to go onstage to say a few words. Our song, "Years In The Making"—inspired by the Raptors' championship-winning season—had just been released, and we planned to open the show by performing it for the first time ever.

Our dressing room was a converted games and leisure room in the hotel. Inside there was a pool table, a bar, and three TVs. All three happened to be set to CP24, the twenty-four-hour news channel. The headlines on the ticker that day had caught our attention, mostly addressing a global matter that I had largely avoided thinking about until that moment. Sometime after six p.m., when we learned that Tom Hanks and his wife, Rita Wilson, had both contracted COVID-19, the tone of the room changed from normal pre-show chatter to nervous laughter. We didn't know what this development meant exactly, but it didn't sound good. Soon there was more breaking news: Rudy Gobert, the centre of the Utah Jazz, had become the first player in the NBA to test positive for COVID-19.

What happened next felt like something out of a movie. Cue the tense flashback montage: the Raptors had just played the Jazz two nights earlier, and a few of the players had been involved in a late game tussle with Gobert. One of them was Serge Ibaka, the player we had just shaken hands with. I stared at my own hands and wondered if there was cause for concern. Moments later, the NBA season was suspended.

One by one I saw the gala's high-flying guests head into corners of the foyer with concerned looks on their faces to make calls. By the time dinner had wrapped up, there was an ominous feeling in the building that couldn't be ignored. Everyone was glued to their phones, as they processed the news in real time and wondered what exactly they should do. Coach Nick, ever the optimist, came into our dressing room to chat about the situation. It was all completely uncharted territory for everyone. We all agreed to buckle up and perform a jaunty thirty-minute set and then hit the road.

By the time we had finished our first song, the players and their families had been whisked out of the room by Raptors security. When Nick joined us onstage, another third of the room was gone. We finished our abbreviated twenty-five-minute set, and whoever had been bold enough to stick around offered a smattering of applause and headed for the exits. We all went home, unsure what tomorrow would look like.

CURVEBALL

When the pandemic arrived, we had to rip up all our plans and begin to make new ones. Unlike some jobs that could be performed remotely from home, or in the field wearing a mask, touring musicians had no choice but to sit idle and wait. At first, I was optimistic the lockdown would only derail us for a few weeks and we'd be back to business in no time. In early March, we had just announced we'd be hosting The Rally for a second time. It was slated for late June in Hamilton. The on-sale was more successful than the first Rally, already approaching twenty thousand tickets sold, and we figured it would be fine with the date more than three months away; the medical experts and health authorities would have everyone back on their feet in time for summer.

During those first few weeks, I spent a lot of time walking the Hamilton Rail Trail, talking on the phone to Ash and Jack. We had no choice but to have a plan for the moment we were given the green light to start playing shows again. To keep myself busy, I started a daily Instagram live series we dubbed "Flatten the Curve Music Class." It was an uncertain time, and most forms of "live" online entertainment that we would come to know throughout the pandemic had yet to be developed. But these online hangs gave my day some shape.

Every day at one p.m., I'd go live and teach whoever else was bored at home how to play one Arkells song. At that point, we had fifty-eight official songs in our catalogue, and I joked with Ash—not believing that we'd be inside for more than a couple weeks—that we'd do this for fifty-eight straight days. As the weeks passed with the lockdown as the new standard, it became clear that I'd easily be able to complete the entire catalogue.

To keep it interesting, I invited special guests to join me from their homes. Tim, Nick, Mike, and Anthony, whom I hadn't seen in person since the gala, all hopped on the chat for a chance to catch up. The line-up was eclectic, including WNBA star Kia Nurse and NHLers Mitch Marner and Morgan Rielly. The Instagram classes ended up being a bright spot in my day and were less about the music lesson and more about the company. My favourite part was the game of chat-roulette that I'd instigate. Fans from all around the world could ask to join the chat, and without any screening or sense of who they were, I'd invite them on to ask whatever questions they had on their mind. Over the course of fifty-eight days, there wasn't one single moment of misbehaviour or hijinks on the live chat. I've always maintained that Arkells fans are some of the most well-adjusted people around, and this experiment proved just that. Local and national news—who were looking for literally *any* good news story outside of cheering on frontline workers—asked for interviews. I somehow did more press in that window of time than I do during most album rollouts.

For the band, the most concerning matter was what to do next. So much of our success came from diligent planning, which was filling a calendar for six to eighteen months ahead. We had just released "Years In The Making" and had planned to roll out the rest of our unnamed album throughout that year. But as time went on, it became clear that releasing new music with no live touring to support it might be a wasted effort. During those early months of COVID, we saw the releases of other bands and artists who had patiently worked on music over the previous few years get lost to the black hole of the lockdown. They'd targeted 2020 as their big year, but those plans changed drastically. Touring has always been an important promotional vessel for a new album, and without any shows for the foreseeable future, it felt hard for our band to get behind any of the spirited, upbeat material we had been working on.

We did our best to read the room and come up with a new plan. We quickly decided that, in our remote setting, we'd work on an intimate acoustic album of our biggest songs.

Over the years, through countless radio station visits where we played acoustic sets, we had developed loose sketches for stripped-down versions of our songs. We knew how they might sound and figured we could find a way to pull off recording the songs, despite being physically apart. We'd call it *Campfire Chords*, and it would be a quiet album for the quietest time on planet Earth. We would release the album in the summertime to keep people company while they hung out in small pods. We hoped it might be the Bluetooth speaker soundtrack for a condo balcony, backyard, or cottage.

Song by song, we sent our parts to Anthony, who assembled the music from home and quarterbacked feedback and suggestions. We had a new song called "Quitting You" that would be the centrepiece, alongside songs like "Knocking At The Door," "My Heart's Always Yours," and "Leather Jacket." I made some secret visits to Anthony's house during those months, and the band eventually got together to put the finishing touches on the album at our pal Aaron Goldstein's studio.

To promote the album, we also needed to adapt. We had already received dozens of offers to do livestream performances, but we'd dogmatically avoided them at all costs. Up to that point, our band had said no thanks to any offer that didn't resemble a real-life show. We didn't want to play at a drive-in theatre with cars honking in appreciation, or a vibeless livestream concert with people watching their screens and listening through their laptop speakers. We didn't want to devalue our live show, the thing that we felt made our band special. Instead, we started assembling a national broadcast special that showcased *Campfire Chords*. We produced the show ourselves. It gave a behind-the-scenes look at the band and where we found ourselves creatively with this new album.

As a pandemic project, our friend Beez was developing an off-the-grid property on a small plot of land up Highway 6, a few hours outside Toronto. Turns out, he, too, needed something to do with his time. Among its many attractive, rustic qualities, the property featured a cool-looking yurt that we thought could be the perfect setting for our "Quitting You" music video, and the ideal backdrop for the *Campfire Chords* special.

In July we did a site visit and made one minor addition: an upright piano purchased on Kijiji. The property perfectly matched the aesthetic of *Campfire Chords*. We wanted to capture the essence of a quintessential summer experience: hanging out with friends and singing songs around a campfire. Unlike other specials we were seeing on broadcast, we could produce something beautiful that didn't remind us of the restrictions of living in a lockdown. It would be a moment to commemorate the strangest time in history at a unique and fitting place. As it all came together, the band chuckled at the irony of the setting: we were playing these acoustic songs together on a beautiful summer day, despite the reality that they had been recorded largely in isolation during the winter.

While I was proud of the impromptu album and the special, it was an undeniably hard time for just about everyone. Within the band, the time apart, lack of routine, schedule, and search for a sense of purpose were enduring struggles. Concerns around leaving the house for something music-related, only to possibly bring COVID home to your family, were constantly being weighed. *Campfire Chords* was released in August, and it accomplished what it aimed to do: keep our fans company with comforting music during a very uncertain moment in time. But more than anything, it provided some structure for the band in a completely structureless time.

RUN IT BACK

Somehow throughout the pandemic, I never felt bored. But amid the make-work projects, we were eyeing the day we could return to the stage. By March 2021, one year after the day the world changed, the vaccine was becoming available and there was a sense that we might be returning to business. We had continued working on the album that would eventually be called *Blink Once* and picked up right where "Years In The Making" left off. We had regular conversations with our team about when we might be able to perform live. Every day, the calls changed in tone, swinging wildly between optimism and despair. We were hopeful that live events would be reinstated, but it was still a shaky time. One day, we heard that the government would allow outdoor concerts with an audience of 25 percent capacity. The next day, we heard whispers of another lockdown.

In July, with good information from officials, we learned that live concerts would be permitted, and we hatched a plan to play the open-air Budweiser Stage at 50 percent capacity the following month. The plan was to announce two shows over a weekend and see what the temperature was amongst the public. It was a vulnerable time for everyone involved, with the media feasting on any mention of a potential superspreader event. Playing the first large-scale concert in Toronto, we knew there could be a target on our back.

The day before the show was to be announced, we were informed that the capacity could be raised to 75 percent (roughly ten thousand tickets a night). Through some combination of our local popularity and people simply dying to go to a concert, we sold through the first two shows immediately and added a third. Capping off the weekend with a Sunday night show, we dubbed the party an "Arkells Long Weekend," as a nod to the three-night stand.

Building the shows—within the constraints of rigid health protocols—required everyone to hit the ground running. Suddenly, after months of sitting dormant, our crew, extended band, and design team had a lot to do in a very short amount of time—four weeks to be exact. By regular standards, this was an ambitious timeline. But in that moment, we had no choice but to figure it out. We commissioned a two-storey, elaborate, one-off set piece inspired by a classic roadside motel sign, which was designed by Mike D. Each night would demand a new wardrobe and updated setlists to satisfy any repeat customers. We'd have a different cover for each night. On Friday, "Dancing On My Own" by Robyn, a nod to the previous seventeen months. On Saturday, ABBA's "Gimme! Gimme! Gimme! (A Man After Midnight)," a song of the moment that had taken over the zeitgeist. Finally, on Sunday, we'd play "(I've Had) The Time of My Life" from *Dirty Dancing* to commemorate the elation we hoped to feel.

By the time our "long weekend" arrived, we had sold almost thirty thousand tickets. In the lead-up to the first concert, there wasn't much time to think about anything but the show itself. With each night featuring more than twenty songs, there was so much material to relearn and so many moving parts to account for. For me, the most important part of the show was the band's entrance. We knew it could be an emotional moment for everyone who missed live music and the magic of a concert. As the lights went down, we displayed a countdown clock on the screens, and the crowd counted down the final twenty seconds together. I had prerecorded a short announcement, reminding everyone to bring their best selves to the night, and then the band hit the stage. People told me later that they cried. Every song that weekend felt like a time-stamp for the moment. We opened with "Years In The Making"; a song originally written about the Raptors' championship run now meant so much more. A new one, "All Roads"—a love song with the lyric "all roads will lead me back to you"—became about the night and everyone there.

Each show was an insane mix of stress, excitement, and catharsis. The memory of our long weekend is something we still hear about regularly from fans. The sea of ten thousand people waving their souvenir rally towels was a breathtaking sight. The loudest cheers of the weekend happened when we welcomed a pair of local doctors onstage who had helped lead the effort to vaccinate Toronto's most at-risk communities. After the delays and postponement of so many weddings over the past two summers, we invited a newlywed couple to replicate their first dance to "And Then Some."

Even our crew and venue staff, who are seasoned professionals, got caught up in the emotion of it all. We all shared tears at various moments. After months of not knowing when or how we'd ever be able to do our jobs the way we once did, we felt so much gratitude to simply be together.

The final show on Sunday night was by far the loosest and most fun for the band. The first two nights were all business, with everyone onstage frantically trying to remember all the parts while appearing to have a good time. By Sunday, we knew we were in the clear and were reminded just how being in a band can be really fucking fun. The night ended with Nick Nurse joining us backstage and presenting us with a celebratory bottle of champagne that Mike D.—in a very uncharacteristically giddy moment—promptly shook up and sprayed all over me.

FREE IDEAS

When we were first signed, marketing was a task assigned to managers and people at the label. Musicians made the art, and the team around the band figured out how to market the music. That always felt a little limiting to me. If marketing is about storytelling, and the goal is to tell the story of our band, who better to tell that story than us?

The more we progressed in our career, the more I wanted us to play point on this part of our business. Over time, our fingerprints would be found all over public-facing ideas. Today, we run our own social media. We come up with our own album campaigns. We design our own merch. We keep our eyes open to fresh ideas, and we find ways to make them happen. This approach foreshadowed the way the music business works today, where artists are responsible for telling their story, largely through social media platforms. The reality is that every touring musician trying to move concert tickets is a brand whether they like it or not. One of our goals was to earn a living from our art, and I wanted to become an expert at getting the word out.

Most marketing ideas start with "What if?" If you are lucky enough to be surrounded by people who like to play ball, your ideas are greeted with an open mind. It's like improv comedy; you need to "yes, and" when you're in the middle of a brainstorm. Some what ifs are bad ideas. I have countless every single day. But even bad ideas are—at worst—fun to talk about and—at best—lead to better ideas that are worth pursuing further.

Marketing might feel like a dirty word to some people in the arts because the term is often associated with faceless corporate branding. And fair enough, so many branding exercises are often contrived, hollow, and look like mercenary work from the outside. But the thing about marketing, which is obvious, though·it often doesn't get acknowledged by artists, is that it can be a truly creative endeavour in itself. Putting together a marketing campaign is a different type of riddle to solve than writing a song, but many of the same principles apply. Is the idea unique? Does it grab you? Does it make you *feel* something? Does it come from a place that's true? These are questions that fire me up when it comes to marketing our art.

In our world, all of our marketing ideas—whether they support a song, an album, or a tour—are about creating something that sparks an earnest connection. As a result, the work we put into marketing our band never feels icky. The broader public is pretty good at sniffing out when an artist is pursuing something dishonestly. An idea needs to come from an authentic curiosity, otherwise you won't have the enthusiasm to see the idea through to the finish line.

The most effective things we've done to get the word out have largely been spontaneous and then executed with precision. And while they might occasionally look premeditated, they are a result of keeping our eyes peeled and the desire to interact with the broader culture. If our band is considered engaged with our audience, it's just because we spend a lot of time asking ourselves, "What if?"

When we released our song "Only For A Moment" in 2018, we wanted to play with the lyrics in the chorus "at karaoke we were trading each verse, you wore my jacket and I carried your purse." So, we rented out a dingy karaoke bar on Yonge Street in Toronto and preloaded the rooms with the new song and a custom karaoke video. The night it was released, we posted a photo of the band at the bar on social media, and on little notice, fans crammed into all those tiny rooms and we belted out the song together.

Later that year, in the lead-up to releasing our song "American Screams," we put up a billboard in Buffalo, New York, with a phone number you could call to get an advance listen of the song before it was officially released. The band filmed the music video in front of the billboard to maximize its exposure. This was before artist campaigns asked fans for their phone numbers. Direct correspondence wasn't as commonplace as it is now. With shifts in technology, there are always new ideas to mine.

On our album release day for *Rally Cry*, we collaborated with Toronto's Union Station and held a pop-up fan market to celebrate during rush hour. The first song on the album is "Hand Me Downs," and we told fans they could come down and recycle their T-shirts by repurposing them as new Arkells merch with our branded printing press. The crowd had first access to the album, and the band ended the event with an unplugged pop-up performance to roughly one thousand people. A packed train station with a crowd singing around an upright piano is how I remember that day. It was the perfect moment to capture the title of the record.

But it's not always this seamless. During the dog days of the pandemic, it felt very hard to do much of anything because the world had stopped. In August 2020, Arkells were set to release *Campfire Chords*, and we understood that traditional marketing exercises (touring, surprise fan interactions, media appearances) weren't available to us. Ash and I would wander around Toronto and pitch each other promotional ideas, and our hit rate was probably less than 5 percent. Everything was impossible to pull off or not worth the hassle.

The week before the album was released, we received a funny tweet from two fans who were driving across the country from Calgary to their hometown in New Brunswick. As a band, we'd done a version of that drive and knew how long and boring those forty-five-ish hours can be.

They asked—on a whim—if they could get an advance copy of the album to keep them company on their long haul. We sympathized with their situation and wondered to ourselves if it was a good idea to send a digital copy of an album that wasn't out yet. Ash is very cautious about handing out music before it's released. I, on the other hand, will give advance copies of unreleased music to just about anyone who asks politely.

Out of curiosity, we tweeted back, asking where they were in their road trip. They told us they'd be crashing in Sault Ste. Marie for the night. By total coincidence, Ash's parents had been visiting Toronto from the Soo and were set to head back home that afternoon.

"What if we burn a CD for them?" I said. Our fans online were now watching this play out, and immediately the idea became that much more fun. We tweeted back with a plan. We told them we'd burn them a copy (which was an archaic chore in 2020), find out what hotel they were staying at, and have Ash's parents drop off the album when they arrived. Even though this was all far more inconvenient and complicated than simply sending them a link to the album, it was way more interesting to us.

Executing these offbeat ideas is where Ash thrives. She loves a to-do list.

Burn the CD. *Check*.

Fancy envelope (that looks good in a photo). *Check*.

Write a personal letter from the band. *Check*.

Coordinate with Ash's parents to not fuck up the plan. *Check*.

Coordinate with the hotel staff. *Check*.

Tweet about it all. *Check*.

When the two friends arrived that night in the Soo, they had our brand-new album waiting for them at the front desk. Success!

But there was a problem. The U-Haul truck they were driving didn't have a CD player. Okay, another social media call-out to anyone who was paying attention to this adventure: "Does anyone in Sault Ste. Marie have a CD player/ boom box for [our new friend]? He hopes to be on the road by 11 a.m. tomorrow. He will mail it from New Brunswick if you need it back." Immediately, we had responses from invested locals willing to part with their dusty, battery-powered CD players—all in an effort to keep this charming journey afloat.

With plenty of whimsy, we understood that there was a good chance print and broadcast media might pick this story up, and they did. Between the social media chatter, the photographable burned CD, and the road trippers live-tweeting their reactions to the songs, the whole affair was very vivid for any viewer and led to coverage on the local and national news.

Of course, the stakes weren't high, and the fate of the album didn't rely on this adventure, but I believe it made a small difference. The story of our band, those travellers, and a burned CD felt like it received more promotion than any traditional album launch could offer. It provided a jolt of unexpected energy during a slow news season. If we're having fun, our fans are having fun too.

All of these ideas are either inexpensive or free and driven completely by the band. All came from the simple desire to have our music heard, with the understanding that in a world where there are tens of thousands of new songs released on streaming platforms every day, it's incredibly difficult to get people to pay attention to *anything* you're doing.

As a result, we try to remain both proactive and reactive. In our experience, being a small business has allowed us to be more nimble and sincere in our marketing. Our version of a "corporate deck" is a daily conversation that is constantly evolving.

Of course, the best marketing for a musician is the art it-self. To write an amazing song. To prepare a live performance that's so exciting and memorable that people go home and want to tell their friends about it. No marketing idea can help an artist who doesn't have the goods to back it up. But if we've made music that we're proud of, the answer to how to promote our work is often right there in front of us.

WIN/WIN

Beyond our own DIY marketing ideas that we tinker with every single day, there are occasional opportunities when you're offered a lift. In February 2018, we had announced Arkells' inaugural hometown festival, The Rally, and there was considerable buzz in our camp about the response from our fans.

Ash and I were at our proverbial battle stations, staring at our phones, scanning social media, and replying to fans who were waiting in a digital queue to buy tickets for the ten a.m. on-sale. If someone has a question about an event or buying a ticket, we want to make sure they can find the answers.

Suddenly, across our screen, we received a notification from a news outlet covering the Winter Olympics in Pyeongchang. It was a video, and we could hear our song

"Knocking At The Door" playing in the background. Turns out, it had become an unofficial theme for Team Canada's medal ceremonies during the games. The song had been released ten months before and had already become a mainstay at sports events, and we were pumped any time it showed up in unexpected places.

"What if we just tweet back something like 'We need to go to Korea and play this for our Canadian Olympians'?" I said to Ash.

Like most Canadians, I enjoy the Winter Olympics and my hopes and dreams—along with the rest of the country's—tend to rest on our hockey teams, figure skaters, curlers, and that one sport where you ski and shoot a gun at the same time.

"Maybe if we add @TeamCanada, they'll fly us over there to do the song for real," I said. Ash added with a laugh: "Tag @AirCanada too. They'll probably do it." Some of the best ideas can start on a lark, and this was one of them.

Air Canada and the Canadian Olympic team saw the tweet and reached out behind the scenes to see if we were serious. The band wasn't on tour, and we told them that we could make it happen, if they were up for the challenge.

There have been many instances throughout our career when brands have approached our band about some kind of promotional partnership, and the conversation itself is always an interesting one. Most times, it's not a fit. The strategy deck they've created isn't aligned with our own goals, and no amount of finessing the idea will make it feel good. We consider their ideas and how we might be included, but more often than not, it's not worth the time and effort to force a fit. The odd time, though, you get to work with a partner and it just feels right. A last-minute trip to the Olympics on the back of one of our songs? *That* felt good immediately.

The next day, the band was together shooting promo content for The Rally at Anthony's apartment. It was all very surreal. I was dressed up as the Hamilton Ti-Cats mascot as I told them what had transpired following our online interactions. I asked if they'd be into the idea of flying to South Korea, and with some mild disbelief, they all agreed. I assured them that at the very least it would be an adventure, which is what I usually say when we are embarking on something that seems outlandish.

Six days later, the band was on a fifteen-hour flight to South Korea to perform for our Olympians.

As soon as we confirmed, we worked with Team Canada to compress what would typically be months of planning into days. The logistics of finding gear, hotel accommodations, and every other travel detail was a tall order. For anyone else involved in the Olympics—media, organizers, and fans—the journey to the games is months, if not years, in the making.

Underneath this rollicking story that found us partnered with an airline and the Canadian Olympic team is some version of marketing. Beyond the centrepiece of our work—our songs and the touring that follows—the creativity required to get the word out is something that can't be ignored. And it can be looked at with derision or curiosity, depending on your attitude. Our band's attitude has always been that we want as many people as possible to hear our music, if for no other reason than because it allows us to keep making it.

As we geared up to head to South Korea, we arrived at Pearson Airport and did an interview with a news reporter who was waiting to see us off. We took photos with the pilots and staff on the plane. The whole conceit—our band heading to the Olympics on no notice, on the other side of the planet—felt both comical and thrilling.

The most intense moment of the trip was arriving at customs in Seoul. We had official documents with us from the Canadian Olympic Committee to prove that we were invited guests, but when you're a musician travelling abroad, border guards can be temperamental. We knew all it would take was one grumpy agent to give us a hard time and put a stop to the entire thing. One by one, each band member and crew had a short conversation with the South Korean agents and were let through. We hopped on a chartered bus to Pyeongchang—and *our* games were about to begin.

Team Canada had full kits that we could wear to the games waiting for us at the hotel. As we rolled through the Olympic village, it kind of felt like *we* were Olympians. I swear, if you put on the Team Canada kit, and you're with a crew of ten people, you become part of the team.

We were there for a total of four days and played three shows for our Olympians, coaches, media, and fans who'd travelled to the games. We ate amazing local food and got to attend a bunch of the events. Figure skating darlings Tessa Virtue and Scott Moir had just won the gold medal for their history-making ice dance performance and joined us onstage to sing along to our cover of "You Make My Dreams (Come True)" by Hall & Oates. We learned that if you want to party with the athletes at the Olympics, it's best to arrive during the last few days of the games because most of them have completed their competitions.

On the way home, our flight was almost entirely full of Olympians, and we felt like phonies wearing our official Olympic jackets, pants, *and* toques as we walked through the airport alongside the athletes. I became nervous and self-conscious about getting eye rolls from the Olympians, but everyone was incredibly kind and thanked us for making the trip and providing entertainment so far away from home.

I've come to understand that the collective impression of our band is made up of thoughtful moments like this. The large majority of Arkells' promotional output is conceived of and executed on our own. We tend to keep brands at arm's length because they can dilute the art and trust that we've worked hard to foster. There is a huge difference between a real authentic experience versus a brand activation, as the latter usually leaves much to be desired. The best brand executives recognize this and let the artist and the partnership shine on their own unique terms. So many of our DIY marketing efforts could be sponsored in some way or another, but we know that impressions for impressions' sake aren't always worth it. But when you have a chance to touch more people than you could on your own, as we did with Air Canada's impromptu volley to get us to Pyeongchang, it feels like catching a wave.

When we returned home, we were left with the feeling that we got the experience of a lifetime, and the athletes and staff were treated to a tailor-made concert to celebrate their years of hard work. I loved being a part of it all. It was a completely organic feel-good moment that made headlines—a total win-win for all.

HALFTIME SHOW

It's rare that you'll encounter a moment when you must summon everything you've ever learned and execute it in one definable act. In 2021, when Arkells were asked to headline the halftime show for the Canadian Football League (CFL) Grey Cup final, we felt like we were ready for the challenge. Our body of knowledge had been built over time, evolving from show to show. After more than a decade of touring and honing our chops as performers, we now had the opportunity to cram everything we knew about showmanship into fourteen minutes in front of millions of people on live television. This all got the blood pumping, so of course, we jumped at the chance.

Since graduating from clubs to theatres to arenas, we had hoped that one day we'd get the call from the CFL for the halftime show. While we'd performed live on television many times before, we understood the scope of this production would be unlike any event we'd been a part of up until now. Past Grey Cup halftime performers included Celine Dion, Justin Bieber, Keith Urban, and Imagine Dragons.

Besides the halftime show itself, so much of the value of the opportunity was the national television and media promotion that comes with being involved in a huge sporting event. From the initial announcement to commercial spots to the media appearances required, we wanted to show the same care and attention for each part of the partnership.

We'd do our best to promote the event—and figured there would be fans of Arkells tuning in—but we also knew there would be a wide audience that was unfamiliar with our music. In addition to the 26,000 people in attendance, there would be millions of people watching the game online and on television. The unacquainted viewers were the ones we started to think about. We'd heard of a stat that television viewers will flip the channel within eight seconds if what they're watching fails to grab their attention. So, when we got the gig, that statistic guided our assignment: how do we keep the average viewer from flipping the channel?

Over the years, as the crowds grew and the shows became longer, we understood that show prep could be an endless to-do list if we wanted it to be. The more we dialled in every part of the performance, the more we enjoyed ourselves onstage and the better the payoff was for the crowd. After some early television appearances, we quickly realized that charisma doesn't ooze through the camera lens in the same way it might in front of a live audience. Great rock bands can often feel flat on television. If you're performing on TV, so much of the magic and impact is entirely dependent on the director and producer in the truck understanding the flow of the performance. Are the camera cuts landing on each musician during the right moment of the song? Is the lighting good? Are the camera angles right? We learned that a memorable performance can be butchered for the viewer at home if you're not communicating with your producing partners to land the right moments.

Preparing for the show started with creating a setlist, but not just any setlist. We understood it needed to be *all killer, no filler*—with a limited amount of time, playing full versions of songs wouldn't serve the show or the audience. We began distilling the best moments of a traditional two-hour Arkells show into fourteen minutes. The setlist wrote itself. We'd start out strong with "Years In The Making"—a nod to our slow and steady career path. Then we'd hit 'em with "Leather Jacket," our biggest song. Next, we'd bring 'em down for an intimate acoustic moment. And then we'd rev right back up with our newest single, "You Can Get It," and close out with "Knocking At The Door" for a final bang.

Once we settled on a fourteen-minute composition, we started to think about blocking. Blocking is the placement and movement of performers in relation to the camera. If you're a rock 'n' roll band, it's not a word you hear much: blocking can be a softer word for *choreography*. The blocking of the show would be key as we intended to make use of three different stages. We'd open on the football stadium turf side by side with the Northern Soul Horns and our backing vocalists, the Arkettes, moving in tandem with handheld instruments as if we were a New Orleans-style brass band. We'd arrive onstage to find bleachers of our fans positioned behind us, singing along to every word. This was strategic. My favourite moment of a show is seeing people sing along, but if you're only capturing the backs of people's heads in the crowd, you're missing that moment on camera. So, we placed them behind us so they could be a part of the performance.

To rehearse for all of this collective group movement, we rented out a basketball gym at Toronto Metropolitan University and taped the floor to represent the dimensions of the space we'd be working with on the field. We had rented out big spaces to prepare for tours, but because we were primarily focused on the audience at home, every detail needed to be mapped out. As we rehearsed, we watched back the single camera feed as if we were a sports team examining game tape.

There were so many moving parts of the show that relied on finely executed camera cuts to pull off the sleight-of-hand tricks for the viewer at home. For example, during the opening shot, the camera had to linger on me on the turf, while the rest of the band scurried onstage and got in position for the big chorus hit. If the camera zoomed out for a wide shot, you'd see the other eleven performers running like their life depended on it. Not good. Every moment of the show was blocked down to the second, but none of it mattered if the camera operators weren't doing what they were supposed to. The rehearsals were one long creative conversation between everyone involved. With camera playback available, we were able to show the production team exactly what we were try-ing to achieve. It's often easier to *show* your collaborators what you want to see, rather than explain it.

We also wanted to offer some surprises along the way, and we understood that each song needed to be a scene change. We recruited our pal K.Flay to come up from L.A. to perform our song "You Can Get It" with us. She's an old friend and loves an assignment. As we explained the nature of the show, she was more than happy to engage in the choreography that we had planned. For the acoustic section, we had the idea to collaborate with The Lumineers, the band that inspired our song "Quitting You." It was a bit of a bold idea, but we reached out and asked if they wanted to share a moment on stage. To our delight, they agreed to come up to Hamilton for the weekend. Jeremiah and Wesley would guest on our song, and then we'd play their hit "Ophelia" together. By the end of November, the show had all the ingredients of some-thing that could be special and memorable. Something that went above what was expected of Arkells.

Despite all of our preparation, on the Saturday, one day before we were set to take the stage in front of a packed sta-dium and millions of viewers, we encountered a hitch in our plans. The weather gods, once again, had other ideas. At work, I tend to smile—almost involuntarily—when things are out of my control. The look on my face isn't quite a relaxed smile. If you're looking closely, it's an expression that is 20 percent smile in my mouth and 80 percent disbelief in my eyes.

Saturday was the allotted day to run our fourteen-minute performance for the Grey Cup *as many times as it took* to get it right. This part of our schedule was critical not only for us but our extended band, the production team, the crew, and K.Flay and The Lumineers, who'd just arrived. After an unseasonably warm Friday in the middle of December, where the weather had been a balmy 12 degrees Celsius, high winds were predicted to be over fifty kilometres an hour on the Saturday. Any activity on the outdoor stage was halted as it was unsafe to be around the lighting and production that had been brought in for the show. We felt stumped. We had been counting on the dress rehearsals to finalize every detail that we had laboured over for the previous month. Without Saturday, the hundreds of hours of preparation felt kind of pointless. So, on Saturday we didn't do much, and I smiled a lot.

On Sunday morning, it was sunny, and the winds had died down considerably. We were allowed a quick dress rehearsal on the field but without the full team of broadcast cameras. We didn't have the benefit of running any of the lighting cues that would be executed during the evening performance, and we'd just have to trust the team to hit those buttons at the right time. It was all nerve-racking. The only point of the rehearsals in the venue was to better prepare the camera operators and people in the truck cutting the live performance.

By the time we were about to hit the stage for halftime that Sunday night, we felt more like a theatre company than a rock 'n' roll band. Despite it all, we were confident. If you've ever participated in a theatre production before, you know the feeling of teamwork and comradery that grows between every person involved. In high school, I had a role in a musical theatre production, and I remember the feeling well. The affection you have for your peers as you work together toward a collective vision is like nothing else.

Our fourteen-minute show felt like it lasted fourteen seconds. I don't remember much. It was all a rush. When we got off stage completely out of breath and fueled by adrenaline, we all asked each other the same question: "Did it go okay for you?" One by one, I learned everyone had a great time up there, and all the beats and cues were hit with precision and ease. Okay, good. We did our part. The next question was if the production crew, with very limited rehearsal, hit their cues. Would some moment that was supposed to be off camera be inadvertently picked up on live television and embarrass the ensemble in some way?

Ash and I headed backstage to find clips online, and we were blown away. After rehearsing in a gym and then in daylight, we didn't really have a sense of how it would all look and feel under the bright lights of a packed football stadium. We scanned through the entire show and were relieved that the production team came through like the true professionals they were. The fireworks at the end were spectacular, so much bigger than we imagined. They nailed just about every moment. The audio team also nailed the mix—ensuring the crowd singalongs were loud and my live vocal was sitting just right.

I later learned that there was a lot of information withheld from me and the band moments before we went on that I'm grateful to have not known. Among other things, it turns out the pre-game show performer didn't have working audio in their in-ear monitors and couldn't hear their backing tracks. The camera on the field that was supposed to cover our opening shot wasn't working and the commercial break needed to be extended to fix it. We were standing on the field waiting to go on, not having any clue what the delay was about. If I had known this before we played, the distraction and concern would've been hard to overcome. The adage is "Ignorance is bliss," but frankly, in heightened moments, it's mandatory.

The success of the performance was the result of so many talented professionals working together. Each department deeply cared about executing their part to perfection. What this experience taught me, and what I've continued to learn, is that large teams need time to gel. Five guys can jam in a garage to practice music, but when the scale of the show and the team grows, it's a bigger boat. You can't turn it too quickly. And when things happen that are out of your control, you need to be ready for that too.

BEING USEFUL

When I was ten, my mum went back to school to become a teacher. At forty-four, she left a career as a freelance graphic designer and followed in the footsteps of her parents, who were also teachers. After the program and her practicums were complete, she was lucky enough to land a job at the closest possible high school to our house, Central Technical School. It's a six-minute walk down the street, and for the next twenty years, Janet Kerman would spend the evenings dutifully preparing for the next day. Marking papers, making lesson plans, calling parents, and packing her lunch.

Central Tech is a big school that offers an array of classes—culinary, art, mechanics—for students who often aren't planning on going to university. It features a massive century-old brick building, with a second building for the art program next to a full-sized football field. There was also plenty of space to take in the kids who couldn't quite make it work in neighbouring schools. If you got kicked out of any downtown school for misbehaviour, there was a good chance you'd end up at Tech. After a few years in the art department, she moved to the special education department and spent the rest of her teaching career working with youth who had learning disabilities.

My mum's classes were often small, sometimes only five to seven kids, and all were students with unique circumstances that led them to her room. I imagine her students would have considered Mrs. Kerman a strict teacher who enforced rules, but no one could accuse her of not deeply caring about the job. As I got older, she'd occasionally mention something troubling that was happening with a student in the classroom or at home. There were a lot of sweet and shy kids in her class, but also many who acted out from the frustration and confusion of their situations. The extra time and attention she gave to her class was second nature and her acts of service have always stayed with me.

By observing my mum's work, it's clear to me who's doing the heavy lifting in our community. It's not rock bands. Like anyone, I can be dazzled by the privileges that my life as a musician has afforded me. I can also get pulled into the vortex of competition and career pursuits, and my mind and attitude risk becoming polluted. I'm aware that any amount of opulence can go to your head quickly. But staying close to the helpers inevitably grounds everything I do. It reminds me of how lucky I am to live in this creative playground all day and of the inherent privilege of the pursuit. The thought of these generous, community-minded people always serves as a nudge. It's a nudge that tells us, as a band, the least we can do is try our best to be useful.

Often the most impactful way to be useful is by using any leverage we've built to connect the dots to get a good idea off the ground. In 2022, ahead of the second Rally, Arkells refurbished a basketball court in one of Hamilton's toughest neighbourhoods and we called it The Rally Court. We put our team-building skills to work, and it turns out that project isn't that dissimilar to any other production we've been a part of. There were budgets to build, timelines to hit, and experts to confer with. We raised the money with partners, created the court design, and worked with the local city officials to make it happen. For people familiar with our band, the name of the court is a nod to Arkells and the hometown festival we created, but 99 percent of the kids from the neighbourhood using the court don't know Arkells had anything to do with it. I doubt that many even know who we are. Yet this project is one of the most meaningful things we've ever done. Every time we drive by, and I see kids using the court, I think of my mum and all the kids she taught at Central Tech.

Part of being useful is understanding that our music can sometimes make a difference in people's lives. It's an unusual duality for me. Even though my favourite songs and bands mean so much to me, it's hard to imagine that our band and our songs could be meaningful to someone else. When a stranger reaches out and tells us how an Arkells song has helped them during some pivotal moment in their life, I'm always genuinely surprised. There are countless stories that fans share via messages, email, or even in comment sections where we learn some of the most intimate and painful moments of their lives and how one of our songs offered some strength and optimism.

Our music has touched communities in ways that continue to surprise me. It's been the soundtrack to striking public school teachers on the picket lines, advocacy groups demanding better from the government, and health care professionals encouraging Canadians to get vaccinated. When you put songs into the world, bonds begin to happen. Arkells have been the soundtrack to many first dances at weddings over the years, and it's an honour to play a small part in the most intimate moment of a couple's big day. If I take a step back, though, I get it. I can't hear Peter Gabriel sing "The Book of Love" without thinking about the people in my life who I love. The right song can often articulate your own feelings with clarity and warmth.

I've learned to accept and embrace this broader sense of usefulness and the responsibility to others. In 2022, we received an email from a thoughtful social worker who worked at McMaster Children's Hospital in Hamilton. She was working with a couple whose eighteen-month-old son had an inoperable tumour and there wasn't much time left. The parents were Arkells fans, and their child loved to dance and groove along to our music. The social worker described how the parents wanted to spend their final days together doing meaningful activities and wondered if we could arrange some tickets to our show down the road in Kitchener. It was important to the parents that their child, who had spent much of his life in the hospital, get the chance to experience live music. We invited the family to soundcheck and started taking requests. Whatever the parents wanted to hear, we would play. At the end of soundcheck, we took photos and exchanged hugs.

The whole experience was profound and emotional for everyone on stage. Anthony and Tim, who were both young parents at the time, saw a version of themselves in that couple. Every single song we played at soundcheck that afternoon and onstage that night took on a different meaning as we sang for the family. Every word became about them: "All roads will lead me back to you," "There's no quitting you," "My heart's always yours." Being able to lend a hand through our songs was a gift and reminded us how music can connect and nurture us through impossible days.

Janet Kerman—who is from a family of teachers and nurses—just wants her son to contribute to the community in a way that is generous in spirit. She is a fan of our music and loves coming to shows—the glitz and glamour is fun for everyone—but I can tell she is most proud when she knows we've been useful.

RELAX, MAX

In early 2023, we played a one-off show in Los Angeles. We got to town on Sunday, three days before the gig. On Monday afternoon, we went to a pool party at a friend's place in Silver Lake. On Tuesday, we had some meetings with our partners at the label. On Wednesday night, we took the stage. A proper trip to California.

After touring plenty the year before and spending time in the studio at the top of the year, it was our first public show in five months. While I usually enjoy myself onstage and feel proud of our efforts by the time the night is over, the windup to almost every show can be a minefield. Despite projecting carefree optimism to the people around me, on tour I am quietly consumed with identifying problems with the show before they happen. I like to think my concern for the work is in part what makes us good, or at least worthy of anyone's attention.

On the week of this show, something felt different: I was feeling more relaxed than usual. I realized that the stress of touring had always been more burdensome than I might have thought. Beyond the physical toll it takes on my body and voice, I tried to understand why it caused so much anxiety. Like many performers, I've tied the success of any given show to my own sense of self-worth. The number of tickets sold was somehow tied to the way people and the world feel about *me* as a person. It can be difficult to separate the art from the person behind it—especially when you are the creator—but it's a reality for anyone whose face, words, and voice are the centrepiece of something that is being sold. I do my best to remember that I am more than my art, and the winds of commercial success are mostly out of my control.

But I also want to be great. I don't spend any time basking over past successes. I'm only concerned with what could be better and if I'm genuinely proud of what we've created. Beyond the larger mechanics of a touring production, there are many details I tend to obsess over on the night of a show. There are endless questions I ask myself.

Are the people in the crowd subconsciously enjoying the atmosphere as much as they possibly can? I labour over the music being played on the PA system before the show. After all, the music between bands *counts*. Like at a dinner party, I want the playlist just right.

When I'm onstage, I might see a familiar adoring fan in the first row, who has seen every show on the tour. Are they getting tired of the same bits and banter that we've prepared to execute seamlessly each night? I feel like I might owe them something special. But, on the other hand, it's possible that they *want* to see the same bit repeated. I don't know their personal tastes, but they occupy my mind.

I think about what I'm wearing. I want to look different than the last time you saw me. I want to be more than the black skinny jeans and plaid shirt that I wore for the first five years with the band. I want to walk onstage and have everyone in the crowd smile at whatever curious, artful, intentional thing I am wearing. If I show up in a boring black T-shirt, I wonder if our crowd would quietly question if I've stopped trying. Will they believe that one of my strengths—overall enthusiasm and care—is beginning to dwindle?

I think about our setlist. Will fans be disappointed if we open the show with the same song as we did on the last tour? Could we have prepared a new last-minute cover to nod to something happening in the zeitgeist? How much do they want the show to feel different than the last time we came to town? When does something cross over from familiar and welcome to tedious and predictable?

I'm "the man with a plan," as Mike D. sometimes calls me, so I feel responsible for how the whole thing goes. I figure if we are going to the trouble of bringing the crew out on the road and investing everyone's time and energy into the show, it better be worthwhile.

In L.A., I consciously tried to allow myself to enjoy the night. I did my best to remind myself that our band—at our baseline—has a body of work and experience that should inspire confidence. We had our entire production team with us and had worked diligently with them to develop a more consistent experience for our live show. We had event-themed merchandise for sale. We had a packed room of fans who were excited to see us.

The whole thing went flawlessly. The crowd was fiery. The sing-alongs were loud. The band played great. And the smile on my face—a smile I often use to disguise my stress—felt genuine.

After the show, somewhere on the walk back to the hotel while we were basking in the glow of the show and looking for tacos, I felt lighter. Ash, sensing a change in me, said optimistically, "You really need to try and enjoy this all a bit more." It was an interesting thing to hear from the person who shoulders everyone else's stress. If our manager—the person who is on the receiving end of everyone's inner monologues and anxieties—is telling me I need to lighten up, I suppose it's something I should continue to investigate.

It's a tricky balancing act, managing the desire to be great, an exposed ego, and the real or imagined stories you tell yourself, but I want to be better at it. I need to be better at it. There's no use spending all this time travelling to these far-off places if I can't enjoy it a bit. Eventually we found a taco truck next to a grocery store parking lot. With the food and the Mexican beer hitting just right, it felt like a day I could build upon.

WHAT'S YOUR ROI?

Return on investment—ROI—is a term I often make fun of, because it's usually used by businesspeople who are so focused on profitability or efficiency that they answer just about every creative question with "Well, what's the ROI on that?" I think it's a foolish term because who's to be the judge of what the greatest ROI is? Payoff for something you did today or a relationship you made last week can happen quickly, but sometimes it takes years. Maybe you'll finish a song that doesn't make the record, but a key lyric becomes the centrepiece of your next big hit. Life is random, as is business, and each little thing you offer to a group might contain some unforeseen value. Little acts are important.

On a Friday night in the summer of 2023, we headlined a festival in Sarnia, Ontario. Right after the show, we slept on a tour bus while driving three hours up the road to Toronto's Pearson Airport because we had to catch an eight a.m. flight to Calgary, Alberta, for another festival in Red Deer the next night. Upon landing, a retired farmer named Gary, who was volunteering for the festival, picked us up in a van and drove us the remaining ninety minutes to our hotel in Red Deer. Everyone was operating on very little sleep, and we were excited for an air-conditioned snooze that would help us recharge from the 30 degree Celsius mid-July heat.

On tour, we had recently got in the habit of setting up ticket "scavenger hunts." Whether we're in Brooklyn or Berlin, this is a practice I try to keep up. On the day of the show, we would leave a few pairs of tickets around town, and I'd make and share a video with hints about where they could be found. Fans who missed getting tickets would go out on the hunt and often shared their adventures on social media. It was a good way to get the word out about the show and hopefully drum up a little extra excitement once we got to town.

In Red Deer, we had already arranged with the local promoter to leave three pairs of physical tickets at the hotel front desk, which, in a digital age, is a bit of an unusual ask that takes some explaining to most promoters.

"Yes. We need them to be physical. No, they can't be e-transferred . . . Please, dear promoter . . . We have a plan."

On the ride to the hotel, I sat up front with Gary the farmer, explained our mission, and asked if he could spare another twenty minutes to toot around town after we dropped off the touring party so we could hide the scavenger hunt tickets. He seemed amused by the idea and had time on his hands. As we drove around Red Deer, he helped me find some good hiding spots—the local college, the recreation centre, and the entrance to the arena where we'd be playing that night—and bemusedly looked on as I took a selfie at each location. Within half an hour, the social media post was up, and I was back at the hotel for a quick nap before soundcheck.

That night, we attracted about three thousand people to the show. We had only played in Red Deer once before, ten years prior when we opened for The Tragically Hip, so the turnout was bigger than I had expected. There were many nice moments throughout the show. It was a perfectly rowdy crowd. They sang loud. They danced. They did all the things we hoped a familiar crowd might do. Despite our ambitious travel itinerary, the band and crew were in great spirits.

I thought about whoever scooped up those tickets and how they might now feel a bond with our band, and certainly more connected to our music than if they hadn't come to the show at all. They saw us cover Dolly Parton's "9 to 5" while I wore a cowboy hat. Great, right? They got to witness the passion of other Arkells fans. They probably told a few of their friends about this bright, unexpected part of their day. We left town with a new belief in Red Deer as a market that we could come back to and grow.

Now, can I be sure that the return on investment for the time spent executing the plan was worth it? I can't. Many choices will remain unquantifiable for a long while, if not forever. But when I think about the decisions I make, I often ask myself, "Well, what's the alternative? What do I want to do with my time? What's important to me today?" I try to be pragmatic, and the ticket scavenger hunt is a small example of an exercise that might contribute to our long-term future.

Other times, you do something on a whim, and the ROI becomes much clearer in the long run. In 2010, for Canadian Music Week, a festival that attracts music industry from around the world, Arkells played a last minute "secret set" at the Rivoli in Toronto at two a.m. We knew there'd be taste-makers in the crowd, and as a new band we wanted to do something extra special to impress them beyond performing our best material. It was a secret because we were going to play an entire set of Motown songs for the first time ever.

My dad went to Wayne State University in Detroit in the 1960s, and we had a lot of music playing in the house when I was a kid. He was also a DJ at the college radio station and would get advance copies of all the big releases. Until the age of twelve, the only music I cared about was The Beatles, The Temptations, and Smokey Robinson. At the time, most indie rock bands of our generation—if they were going to do a cover song—would opt for something guitar based like Neil Young or The Clash. I thought it would be interesting if we did something none of our peers were doing.

It took a lot of work to prepare for the night, as we were a young band in the middle of a heavy touring schedule. We learned twelve songs: everything from Stevie Wonder to The Supremes. At midnight, a line of people formed down the block. The show was a crammed, drunken, sweaty affair. It ended up being one of the most memorable and buzzed-about sets of the festival. It was a whole new creative assignment for us, but by the next morning we were glad that we had taken on the experiment, even if it was just for one night.

But it didn't end up being just for *one night*. From there, an Arkells *secret cover set* became part of our reputation: a revered but seldom seen part of the band's identity. In the beginning, we rarely performed the set as a public show, but if Arkells were invited to play at a music industry party, with a less familiar crowd, we knew it would bring the house down and leave a lasting impression. Instead of a full set of original songs, we might pepper in a couple of our singles and then bust into a full set of raucous covers. In a very competitive industry, we quickly understood that having a one-of-a-kind cover set up our sleeves was one of the ways our band could set itself apart. To this day, music industry folks still remind me of the first time they saw us do covers in some tiny club years ago.

The ability to be musically nimble always pays off. Mastering those covers led to all kinds of fun we were not expecting. And as the band's own catalogue and fanbase grew, we began getting more offers to play private events. During a party at the legendary Horseshoe Tavern, the pop star Kesha once hopped up and sang along, unprompted. British mogul Richard Branson has danced along in the crowd for a show during the Toronto International Film Festival. Hockey legends have jammed to their favourite songs at NHL parties and then invited us to their games.

Private events are always curious because of the varied people in the crowd. We've played for optometrists, lawyers, accountants, unions, and a range of brands. There might be a twenty-something in the audience who is a diehard Arkells fan, but there might also be a fifty-five-year-old secretary who has never heard of us. In these situations, we realized it was best to take off our "artist" hats and put on our "entertainer" hats. These shows are not an Arkells concert; they are a company party. I've had many conversations with musicians about these kinds of gigs because they're not necessarily easy. Most artists who have made a career performing their own music feel somewhat ambivalent when hired to be the company entertainment. The experience can be humbling because you're not playing for a room of dedicated ticket holders.

Recognizing we've been hired to do a *job* is a small shift in mindset that has helped us enormously. When we walk onstage, we've learned to remain undeterred if the audience seems unsure what to make of us. From years of touring, we've collected so many tricks to win them over by the end of the night. I tell personal stories, prepare bits, and really try to get to know the crowd. We'll hit 'em with some Stevie Wonder and Hall & Oates and then venture off into ABBA, Bruce Springsteen, and Taylor Swift. It's a point of pride for our band that we have learned to handle ourselves in these moments and deliver the best possible show that the attendees could hope for. Like everything else we do, we want people to feel like they got their money's worth and more.

Private events, like the ones I'm talking about, not only make new fans but help fund the future art itself. This is ultimately why we do it. Every time we book a private show, we invest that money back into the operation—whether that's the making of our next record, expanding our touring crew, or better stage production on our next live run.

There are some investments I can easily draw a line from to see their return. I know the payoff of writing a song will come with playing it onstage for years to come. But the more interesting returns come in more abstract ways. The stranger in Red Deer might become a fan for life. The cover set became a significant part of our business into the future. Again and again, past projects and experiences re-enter my creative life in valuable ways, often when I least expect it. Lessons that I learned ten years ago continue to be reshaped. Putting together a business plan is important, but the intangible moments of action can be too.

THE FEELING

It happens every time. A moment of emptiness comes, usually somewhere between the 175th to 250th listen to a new song we are working on, when the excitement of having brought an idea to life starts to wear off. The feeling it has offered me, the hunch that I might be onto something special, and the chase of trying to make it sound as good as it does in my head aren't giving me the same high, and it's time to move on to the next idea. It usually means I've taken an idea as far as I can.

This is just one of many big feelings that come from being involved in any kind of creative pursuit. There are highs, and there are lows. Working on music can be one of the most challenging and confusing things we do, but it's also the most personal and deeply satisfying. After meandering around in the darkness, the feeling of stumbling into a creative answer we've been searching for—whether it's a lyric, drum pattern, or guitar melody—is hard to replicate.

One of my responsibilities in the band is to get a sense of what everyone wants to do, how they can best thrive creatively, and then plan accordingly. The nature of a five-way creative relationship is that it will always be imperfect, and depending on the assignment, someone will end up feeling less than satisfied. But there is trust that we are all rowing in the same direction. As we've gotten older, the guys have become very patient with my creative rhythms and supportive of my style of work. I am an imperfect leader in many ways, but I do my best to listen and anticipate what the guys are yearning for. I have many blind spots, but understand that the success of the band relies on their insights and instincts.

While we were touring in 2022, Mike D. expressed the simple desire to get together and jam with no goal or timeline in mind. We wrote our early records that way—jamming together in a room—and he thought it'd be good to try working that way again, as he enjoyed the process and the results. He also specified that he didn't want us to be in a rush. He probably mentioned this because I am known to usually be in a rush. I might call it "excitement."

Our more recent records had been made a bit differently. I had encouraged us to jam *less* and get right into the studio and just start figuring things out as we went. I had concluded this was the best way forward because I had come to believe that in the early stages of songwriting, your first instinct can often be the best one. I had listened to early demos of songs from *High Noon*, and an early take of "11:11" ended up sounding basically like the final version, at least to my ears. I wondered if we had wasted months needlessly running the song in our jam space, when the first idea sounded complete. Other recent recording experiences, like "Knocking At The Door" and "Quitting You," that had come together quickly felt like some of our most innovative and exciting musical turns.

While I love the early music we made together, and the adventure of it all was undeniably remarkable, it's the occasional moments of tension from that time that have stayed with me. Each of the guys would have their own memories of recording, but the prevailing feeling for me was of quiet anxiety. I wanted to be great, and I wanted us to all get along. We were touring 150 to 200 days a year. We had little money. The future was very uncertain. We were in our mid-twenties. We were firing managers. In the studio, we were a young group capable of passive-aggressive looks and bitchy comments as we tried to express ourselves and get what we wanted out of each song. Those early years of dialogue and behaviour shape all conversations, for better and for worse. Ask any band that's been at it for long enough—the relationship usually resembles a five-headed marriage.

So, I began to investigate my own emotions and ask myself why I had reservations about the desire to return to jamming out new songs. I had grown comfortable getting in the studio with producers who were a little heavy-handed with their ideas and direction. I felt that, after a handful of albums under our belts, they could push us further. As a songwriter, I had become somewhat bored and unimpressed by my own abilities and learned new tricks every time I worked with someone new. But I knew returning to the original approach was important to the guys. We'd all evolved in our own ways since the early days.

But beyond any interpersonal reflections I was having about my band's marriage, I realized there was something else even more telling: I simply *hated* most jam spaces. We haven't had one since the *High Noon* sessions. Historically, jam spaces are located in some industrial part of town where rent is a bit cheaper and there is ample space for gear and making noise. Usually, in this version of hell, you're in a windowless dwelling, crammed in a room between other groups working through terrible covers of "Sweet Child O' Mine," or their newest death metal composition. Not to belabour the issue, but trekking out to a jam space in the middle of nowhere would ruin my creative flow. I hate, and I mean *hate*, sitting in cars. Further, where are the good coffee shops? The point is, the more I thought about it, the more I realized that maybe my allergy to band jam sessions had to do with my historical relationship to the physical jam space itself. I don't want for much—but routine is just about the *only* thing that's important to me. So, I started to see what alternative spaces might be available.

I quickly found a friend's nearby-ish space and booked it for an initial three-day session. A week before we were set to get together, I got a call from the owners saying that it was accidentally double-booked, and Arkells were out of luck. I then did what I should've done from the beginning. I asked myself, "Who is the most successful musician that I know in town, and where do they rehearse?" I texted Ed Robertson from Barenaked Ladies.

BNL have a storied career that has lasted over thirty years. They had a number one hit in America in the 1990s and have worked consistently since. I saw them when I was sixteen and have been a fan all my life. When Ed reached out a few years ago asking if he could come to an Arkells show with his family, I was delighted. He has a keen sense of humour and has been supportive and generous with our band. Ed texted back immediately and said they often get together at "Jim's place." I perked up. Jim is Jim Creeggan, the smiling red-headed bassist of BNL who lives a few blocks from my house. Ed gave me Jim's number, and within an hour I was standing in Jim's backyard studio.

Nick, Ash, and I were given a short tour of his homespun facility. I was frankly blown away by what I saw. It was the opposite of everything I hated about jam spaces. Natural light. No dirty carpets. No cigarette stench. There was a grand piano that made bad piano players like me sound like professionals. Jim explained that he'd never rented out the space, but it was "for the neighbourhood." *For the neighbourhood? What does that mean?* He explained that musicians from the neighbourhood often use it, and since I lived in the neighbourhood, he was happy to host Arkells as we worked on some new music.

Not far from Jim's place was Trinity Bellwoods Park, where I had sat in the rink guard hut all those winters ago, trying to figure out how to write my first songs. I texted the band to let them know we had found a great place to work, and just like that, all my apprehensions about getting together to jam disappeared.

A three-day session turned into three months. We weren't in there every day, but I sheepishly asked Jim for three- to four-day windows that might work around his schedule. He was also working on songs for the next BNL record and explained that our creative energy was good for him too. While we jammed out songs in the big room, Jim would be in the control room recording acoustic ideas of his own. A few times a day he would pop his head out and offer us words of encouragement.

During these sessions I tried my best to be mindful of my body language. I reminded myself that there was no time-table. While I can often be a poor communicator if something isn't landing the way I want, I knew I needed to have less of an opinion in the early creative stages. I needed to let every-one wrap their heads around the material at exactly the speed that made sense to them. There were lots of great ideas in the room waiting; we just had to look for them. From there, so much magic happened.

I had been writing a lot, and unlike much of our material, which aims to be spirited and anthemic, all the new songs were personal, raw, and reserved. They were all heartbreak songs, quiet little conversations I'd been having with myself. Originally, the plan was to work on one new original song to add to an acoustic version of *Blink Once* and *Blink Twice* called *Blink Nice* (we'll do it one day), but once the band got working on the new material, it took over our attention and energy. As the list of songs written down on the small white-board started growing, Nick said with a grin, "Looks like we have a new record." What was supposed to be a casual hang turned into something that felt like an important creative exercise for all of us.

As we sunk into the material in the middle of winter, the songs had a pace and vibe that made me feel stoned by the end of the day. Anthony would take the ideas home and re-cord string arrangements and add other production to songs that were largely live-off-the-floor performances. Mike sent a beautiful piano composition called "Quiet Love" that I wrote melody and lyrics over. Without an agenda, Tim and Nick played with a tender sense of patience and personal expression. The record wound up being called *Laundry Pile*, and even though in many ways it's the outlier among our records, in other ways it feels the most *us*. It was the record we needed to make at the time, and those jam sessions yielded some of the most rewarding experiences I've had making music with the band.

I learned a lot being around Jim during those months, too, but what resonated the most is that there is no greater excite-ment and anticipation than being at the beginning of a new project. As Jim prepared for the next Barenaked Ladies album, his enthusiasm for the new songs and the prospect of work-ing with his bandmates brought up the same kind of eagerness you might expect from a young artist making their first re-cord. Jim is sixteen years older than I am, but he acts like a sixteen-year-old when he's talking about music. I want to hold on to some version of that feeling forever.

Sometimes music fans might wonder why artists who've had long careers continue to make music when they don't have to. Why write another song when you already have a huge catalogue and the time to do literally anything else? Why write a song when it might not be heard by as many people as you'd hope? Why bother with the care and compromise required to be part of a group when you could just do it on your own? What people don't understand—and what took me a while to grasp—is that there is nothing like the diversity of feelings that every stage of the creative cycle can offer.

For any enthusiasm I have when *starting* an idea, I am equally enthusiastic to have the idea sharpened. I get high off the contributions of others. Making things would get pretty stale and boring if it was just me doing it all by myself all of the time. When a bandmate comes through with a great idea or executes a part perfectly, I get the same feeling I do when I'm playing pickup basketball and my teammate hits a game winner. The ball rattles through the hoop, the entire team yells "Fuck yeah!" and pumps their fists. The commercial fortunes of the art are completely beside the point and don't exist when you're creating. When you're working with people who care and come with the right attitude, it's the push and pull of group work that is the reward itself.

There is nothing more exciting than listening back to an idea that you *know* has some potential. And yet there's nothing more deeply frustrating than the period when the song is failing to live up to the potential you hear in your head. Once you go through it all with your collaborators and finally hear the mix with everything in its right place, it's such a satisfying feeling. And then there's nothing emptier than when that feeling wears off. And that's why, when the timing is right, you start the chase all over again.

SETTING THE SCENE

With each passing album, tour, or "era," the concept of re-invention becomes more of a focus. At the heart of reinvention is storytelling. Everything we do—and I truly mean everything—is a story. One that you get to write, and then rewrite again and again. It's one of the most invigorating parts of being creative. Whether it's a song, a show, or a wardrobe choice, you're trying to tell a story that is different from the last.

Arkells have been fortunate to have many bucket-list experiences, which have grown in scope or quality over time. We've created a hometown festival, toured all over the world, and made music with countless talented collaborators. As I think about what comes next, I try to be mindful of what made the last experience special and how I can keep the next one fresh. How do we outdo the last one? We evolve, we learn, and we know we need to take chances.

As a band, we put a lot of care into reinventing our live show with each tour. When I imagine the arc of our show, there are certain goals to achieve within the set. We like to start big, before introducing each band member. It's a high energy show, but we also allow moments to breathe. We want to blow their minds with a surprise and then have two more aces up our sleeves.

As much as I belabour choosing the setlist, that part kind of writes itself. The setlist is the script for the story you're about to tell. The more interesting part is reinventing the moments *within* the songs. Playing the songs themselves, I know we can do. But envisioning our songs as canvases for little scenes is how we shake it up. When fine-tuning a story becomes the mission, every interaction might lead to something more memorable. Sixteen years after we put out our first album, something happened onstage one night that we'd never encountered before.

In June 2024, on the first night of a weekend stand at Budweiser Stage in Toronto, we were about to debut a new scene for the crowd. As we introduced what should have been a blazing piano solo from Anthony, his keyboard stopped working in front of a sold-out audience. With the band surrounding him, like breakdancers waiting to take their turns, we all stared at an electric piano that had suddenly conked out.

Establishing this scene was my job. I had devised a direct and slap-happy way to dramatically set the stage for Anthony's solo. With his big thick-rimmed glasses and his punk rock physicality, Anthony has always possessed a sense of comedy and fun to his piano playing. He is *expressive*. He puts his feet on the keys, slams the piano with his fists, and sticks out his tongue as he goes. We've always built a scene around his solo.

We can always feel it when the time has come to shine up an old bit though. With weeks leading into the rehearsals for this tour, I had spent a lot of time thinking about this particular part of the show. I spent hours on YouTube trying to find inspiration from everything from the Marx Brothers to the E Street Band to Little Richard. I had dozens of conversations with Anthony, the band, and crew trying to reimagine a bit we'd performed for years.

This raucous instrumental bit is an early moment in the show, positioned to display some personality. It allows everyone onstage and in the crowd to let their guard down and loosen up. Anthony is such an electrifying pianist, and the moment I turn it over to him is one of my favourites.

On past tours, Anthony has blazed through solos from recognizable songs or had instrumental standoffs with other band members. The storytelling lets the music settle in, and while the tension grows, the focus of the crowd is directed entirely on the man of the moment.

We rehearsed the choreography around this solo for four days with the full band, detailing all the musical flourishes and stage blocking that would build the moment to a euphoric musical conclusion.

On the night of the show, over Tim's drumbeat, I'd explained to the crowd that our Anthony—despite his glasses and large keyboard rig—was no nerd! Even though the piano might not be considered as "cool" as other instruments, Anthony was in fact the musical leader of our group. "When Tony says, 'Jump,' we say, 'How high?'"

With thousands of people watching, as I introduced his moment to shine—his keyboard only offered silence. For the first twenty seconds—which felt like twenty hours—I just stood there next to Anthony, smiling, waiting for the answer to reveal itself. Seconds passed. Mike D. approached the rig and pretended to fiddle with a knob. Despite all bandmembers cracking a smile or laugh in disbelief, the tension kept rising. With no other choice, the band started to kill time. Tim and Nick kept the rhythm, the Northern Soul Horns started to vamp, and I put my arm around Tony, wondering exactly what we were supposed to do.

Then out of nowhere, a superhero appeared. Our drum tech, Miami Matt, swooped in from the wings with a new keyboard under his arm and quickly began unplugging things. We had no idea our drum tech knew anything about Anthony's complicated setup. How did Miami appear so quickly, inserting himself like lightning into a tableau that felt as if it was moving in slow motion? Within forty-five seconds, Anthony's rig was working again, and the entire band knew exactly where we'd left off, without missing a beat. The moment was so riveting that people wondered if it was all scripted. The drama of it all was my favourite part of the night.

The funny part is it was loosely scripted—but intended to tell an entirely different story. For the crowd, it felt like the highlight of the night. The scene was captured on socials and viewed over a million times that week. Miami Matt became a legend in the comments. A unifying moment.

With a good story, the teller and receiver both get something out of it. Sometimes I imagine our band as a theatre production with a half-written script. And maybe that approach is what makes the job remain fresh. With every show, we take the care and attention to build a scene, while holding on to the flexibility and confidence to let the beats of each scene reveal themselves. If you're not engaged, it's easy to fumble the assignment: I've watched some bands play twenty-minute sets that felt like they'd never end. We want to make our two-hour show feel like it flies by.

The day after, a very common question I was asked was "When the keyboard broke, was that planned? How were you not totally freaking out?" I laughed. Quite the opposite! We'd planned an entirely different bit, and a new story wrote itself that night. In the moment, I didn't freak out for a second. I had a hunch it might turn into the best moment of the show. And it did. It starts with simply being open and present to every moment, so you can get swept away.

HUNGRY HEART

My dad has always loved going to the movies. There was a period in my youth when he seemingly skipped work for a full week in September to attend two to three movies a day during the Toronto International Film Festival (TIFF). He and a friend would draft all the movies they were going to see for the week, and he'd leave at nine a.m. and be gone for the day. His father, David Kerman, was a film and stage actor, and his mother, Bunny, was a TV writer, so growing up he was surrounded by an appreciation for storytelling and performance. As a teenager, he had a formative experience at the movies that inspired a ritual he's practised ever since.

It was 1968, and my dad was back in New York City visiting his family. He'd been away at university in Detroit and had some time to kill in the afternoon while his folks were at work. He went to the theatre and saw a movie called *Rosemary's Baby*. He explained to me that he went into the movie knowing literally nothing about it. If he had read one review or even seen the movie poster, he would've known that someone was going to give birth to a demon baby in the film. But he went in cold, and it allowed him to follow the plot without any expectations. When the main character revealed that she'd been impregnated by Satan himself, it knocked him right over. He remembers the chills that ran up his spine. What a rush! From that moment on, he was hooked—not just on movies but on not knowing anything about their plots. This strategy has worked many times since. Once at TIFF, he saw a movie featuring two cowboys in the mountains. At first, he figured it was a classic Western, but before long the two hunks were kissing and falling in love. Every other person on planet Earth who went to see *Brokeback Mountain* knew it was gay cowboy movie. Not Mike Kerman. My dad still holds on to that sense of awe he had when he was eighteen.

To this day, he's remained somewhat pathological about movie spoilers. It drives my mum nuts. They'll be making polite conversation at a dinner party, someone will innocently bring up a new movie they enjoyed, and the mood changes instantly. My dad will make a weird face and blurt out, "Please don't say anything else! Or at least let me leave the room first." The participants will be confused, and my dad will exit the exchange and come back when the movie talk is finished. If you go to the movies with my dad, he might ask you to give him a little nudge when the movie is starting, because during the trailers he closes his eyes and puts on his headphones. I'll sometimes look over and see his shoulders bopping while he mouths along to a Bob Marley song to distract himself.

This quirk—if you'll allow me to call it that—comes from a good place, in my opinion. And one that I can relate to. It's a quirk born of passion. He remembers the feeling of seeing a movie without knowing anything about it, and he's determined to experience it again. His strategy allows him to interact with art in a way that excites him.

One recent January night at three a.m. when he couldn't fall asleep, my dad began to watch a new Netflix documentary made by Robert Downey Jr. called *Sr.* about his father, the decorated filmmaker Bob Downey. The movie is a beautiful portrait of a complicated father and the relationship with his work and family. Colleagues and admirers interviewed in the documentary describe the daring nature of Bob Downey's storytelling and point to his film *Putney Swope* as an illustration of his sense of humour and social commentary about race in America. *Putney Swope* is about an ad agency on Madison Avenue and begins with the boss dying at the boardroom table of a heart attack. In *Sr.*—the documentary—they feature that exact clip, where the boss keels over in front of his executive team. The scene is incredibly over the top, with the boss delivering his death with the zeal of a comedic Shakespearean actor. Who was the actor playing that small role for about a minute of the film? David Kerman. Imagine that. My dad, in the year 2023, at three in the morning, watching a documentary on Netflix made by Robert Downey Jr.

about *his* father and then sees his own dad on the screen in a movie made in 1969. What a thrill!

David Kerman passed away when I was very young, but there are pictures of us together and I have some distant memories of being around my grandfather. He was a working actor his entire life, performing in everything from TV shows to movies to commercials and off-Broadway theatre productions. He modelled for print ads and did voice acting.

My dad said that even with his eclectic resumé, his father felt some sense of disappointment about the way his career ended up. It always seemed like David Kerman was one break away from making it big. He'd land supporting roles in TV shows but never the lead.

Despite any career disappointments or shortfalls my grandfather may have held onto, my dad explained that his father was always propelled by the craft of acting. He worked late into his life and found ways to stay busy and engaged in the work. He never made a ton of money but always enough to support his family. In fact, he enjoyed acting so much that when he had downtime toward the end of his life, he'd volunteer to do run-throughs and table reads for new theatre productions in search of talent to workshop material.

We tend to delineate between the lives of an amateur and a professional, or a bestselling creative and a little-known entity, but we all have so much more in common than we realize. I see myself in David Kerman. He was determined to take on all kinds of acting gigs—that were creative and engaging in their own ways—to continue working and being employed in a very competitive field. At the heart of it is passion. Life outcomes are random, but your passions are not. And they should be fed and nurtured.

Even though I feel ambitious about my work and hope our songs and shows can find an audience, it's the love of the creative process that fills my cup. Naked ambition feels empty. Passion, on the other hand, gives way to a deeper, more consuming feeling. The stress you experience from wanting to do a good job in your art is wrapped up in joy and wonder. On the other hand, the stress from sales and critical reputation of your art is wrapped up in your ego. Two very different things.

I often get asked, "What's your favourite show of your career?" I think the asker assumes I'll say one of the big ones—say, headlining an arena. But I never have a good answer. It all depends on if I think we were prepared for the night and we executed our vision. If we felt connected and understood by the crowd. To this day, when someone congratulates us on a show we just played, whether it's for 25,000 people in Hamilton or 500 people in Munich, I simply say, "We'll take what we can get." While I love my job so much, I also understand that I am not entitled to the next phase of my career. It's this keen understanding that keeps me creating.

NOT THE LAST CHAPTER

With any creative project, you can try to plan things out, but like in life, you can only plan so much. There are so many experiences and things you will learn along the way that will shape your desire and shape your work. The thing you thought you wanted? You might find you simply don't care that much about it anymore. Conversely, a new source of entertainment may emerge, and if you consider it—move toward it—you might wind up in a place you couldn't have imagined.

Earlier I mentioned that writing a book seemed like a stupid thing for me to take on because I didn't know if there was much to say, and more importantly, I doubted if I had the interest or resolve to write one. I've always thought of myself as a "short spurt" guy, and writing a book is the opposite of that. It's a very long process that requires patience.

But as I've worked on this book on and off over the past two years, I've learned new things about myself and my mind. Even the parts of writing the book that I assumed I'd dislike, like the editing, turned out to be enjoyable and even fun sometimes. It's kept me company in the mornings at the coffee shop. It's kept me distracted when I'm on a turbulent flight. It's been a new part of my day with Ash. As we go for our morning thinking stroll, I read her an excerpt of something new that I just wrote. Yes, I need to perform, even if it's just for an audience of one giggling person. You can make an author out of a lead singer, but he'll remain a lead singer.

I have two friends who write full-time, and I thought about them often as I worked. My childhood friend, who reads and writes more than anyone I know, was working on a script and on one occasion was so consumed by the work that when I asked him to pick up some chips and snacks for a party we were going to, he said he didn't have time. Even though it was a sleepy Sunday night, more writing needed to be done. This was very annoying to me in the moment, but I smile now looking back on it. His happy place is writing. It's not the business or the networking or anything else. The way he wrestles with the words on the page to express his ideas—and the act of getting them just right—feels more aspirational than most jobs I can think of and strikes me as one of the purest forms of connection.

I have another friend, an internationally bestselling novelist, who was a sounding board throughout my writing process and answered every dumb question I had with enthusiasm. I sent her a first draft, and she read it and offered notes. Later,

I read back some of the writing and was completely mortified I had shared it in the first place. It felt like a fifth grader had written it. Her response: "Do *not* be mortified, you know I thought it was great. Also. A first draft is never about the sentences or the quality of the writing. It's about the content and the voice! I promise you my first drafts feel the same. Even down the line, after all the revising is done, I do a whole edit just thinking about how to make the writing-writing better. I find editing so satisfying and think you will too."

What amazing advice. Her zeal for writing made *me* like writing more, somehow.

I am very much a novice, but I love thinking like a writer, and I've picked up so many great lessons on the craft itself. Working with an editor reminded me a lot of working with a music producer, where the creative choices are a conversation. One party suggests an idea, the other might have questions and push back, and the more you're able to express how you feel about the idea—and then test it out—the sharper it should get. Even something as solitary as book writing can be way more collaborative than you'd imagine.

I hope this book is a small reminder that the act of participating—or continuing to find new ways to participate—is the point. Exactly what rewards you reap will remain undetermined until you get out there and exercise your creative muscles. Sometimes it's a connection with an artistic partner, like the feeling I get when I'm passing songs back and forth between the guys in the band. Sometimes it's learning something brand new from a producer and working in a way I've never thought to before. Sometimes it's throwing a concert and bonding with strangers through a story you've prepared and a production you've built. Sometimes, when all plans go sideways, it's the satisfying three a.m. slice of pizza you pick up on the way home after you've been to hell and back.

With writing, I have something I can do during the quiet moments of the day and quiet moments of the year. The unexpected gift of this experience was the new path it revealed. It's a portal to a creative world I can enjoy outside of music. Being in a band means you're often dependent on a much larger apparatus to structure your life. Now I have an outlet that is simply my own. The beginning of January and the end of August don't frustrate me anymore.

Creativity isn't a zero-sum game. I've come to learn that seemingly unrelated projects can spark ideas and help shape the next. For me, the diversity and the scope of work helps keep me energized. Whether I'm bouncing between writing, playing piano, or planning our next event, I never feel too burnt out because the moment I lose perspective on one idea, I can put it aside and tinker with another.

Like listening to our albums, after this book is out, I might pick it up and read the words and wonder, "Who was this guy?" When you create something, it's a time-stamp of who you were that day. In time, I don't even have to agree with any of the creative choices I made in this book. And I suppose it's interesting for that reason itself. The foreign feeling of those past words only means I'm immersed in the next thing, searching for the next jolt of excitement. I want to make any given day a contender for the "glory days" conversation.

I want a life so busy and immersive that I couldn't even tell you what the best chapter was.

When you start any creative endeavour, you have an idea of where you want to go and what you want to accomplish. Those goals are important and provide something tangible to help propel you. You might achieve them, or you might not. But what I've learned is that you don't accumulate those experiences as if they are souvenirs to put in your house or some trophy to prove you did something. They are only there to provide meaning and context for what you do today.

ACKNOWLEDGMENTS

I never would've finished this book if not for Ashley Poitevin's persistence. Well, I might've finished it, but it would've been far less good. I get lazy toward the end of most projects, just wanting them to be wrapped up and done. Not Ash! Through our conversations, she offered so many great ideas and tweaks, and is a true creative herself.

My memory of writing this book will be all the neighbourhood coffee shops that caffeinated the morning writing, and then editing with Ash in the afternoon—pulling up the Word doc on the TV screen, reading aloud as she fixed things. I'd lie lazily on one end of the couch, often eating Thai food, while she'd have the computer on her lap, making adjustments. I don't think this is how most writers do it, but they're missing out. May everyone find an Ash in their life.

To my editor Laura Dosky, thank you for steering this book, this ship, the right way. Your encouragement from the beginning instilled so much confidence. You always asked just the right questions, allowing me to zoom out and re-member what each section was, in fact, *about*. In an editor, I've learned, you want someone who always makes you feel incredibly smart, while gently correcting the countless errors in your writerly judgement.

To the entire team at Penguin Random House Canada, it's very cool to say to friends and strangers, "Yeah, I have a book coming out, soon . . ." and then casually drop, "with Penguin Random House. *Ever heard of it?*" Thanks for teaching me the ropes of the publishing world and for the free copies of your world-class books every time I stop by the office.

To my creative family, I'm humbled to work with such talented and caring professionals—the list of contributors is in the hundreds. The creativity and daily problem solving required to build a career in music is truly a team effort. I feel invincible when I hit the stage because Arkells have you in our corner.

To my friends, who've all taken starring roles in my life at various times. I think about how vital each friendship became, and how it made every experience so much more meaningful because we got to share it. For those of you who weren't namechecked in the book, I know what you're thinking. How did *that guy* get mentioned, and not me? To that I say, blame Laura! The book was much longer in the beginning, with stories featuring every single one of you, but she insisted on editing it down. At one point, you each had a chapter, I promise. I would personally send you those chapters to read and enjoy—nothing would make me happier—but sadly those files were lost in the Great Penguin Random House Fire of 2024, and never recovered.

To the band, thanks for sharing this grand experiment with me. By the time this book comes out, we'll be approaching the twenty-one-year mark. Here's to another hundred.

To my sister Emily, who's been my biggest cheerleader since day one. You're full of joy, optimism, and resilience, and you're an inspiration to our entire family. To my mum and dad, I imagine the trick to parenthood is finding the right amount to care about your children. Not enough, and the kids will have issues. Too much, and they're also in trouble. You've hit the sweet spot. Thank you for everything.